MW01119415

Using Windows NT:
The Essentials for Professionals

Marshall Brain

Kelly Campbell

P T R Prentice Hall
Englewood Cliffs, New Jersey 07632

Library of Congress Cataloging-in-Publication Data

```
Brain, Marshall.
    Using Windows NT : the essentials for professionals / Marshall
    Brain, Kelly Campbell.
      p.  cm,
    Includes index.
    ISBN 0-13-091977-2
    1. Operating systems (Computers) 2. Windows NT. I. Campbell,
    Kelly (Kelly D.) II. Title.
QA76.76.063B718  1994                              93-4999
005.4'469--dc20                                       CIP
```

Editorial/production supervision and interior design: *Dit Mosco*
Cover design: *Tom Nery*
Cover photo: *Super Stock,* Lynn Valley, North Vancouver
    British Columbia, Canada
Manufacturing buyer: *Alexis Heydt*
Acquisitions editor: *Mike Meehan*

 ©1994 by P T R Prentice Hall
Prentice-Hall, Inc.
A Paramount Communications Company
Englewood Cliffs, New Jersey 07632

The publisher offers discounts on this book when ordered in bulk quantities. For more information, contact:

> Corporate Sales Department
> PTR Prentice Hall
> 113 Sylvan Avenue
> Englewood Cliffs, NJ 07632
>
> Phone: 201-592-2863
> Fax: 201-592-2249

All product names mentioned herein are the trademarks of their respective owners.

Printed in the United States of America
10 9 8 7 6 5 4 3 2 1

ISBN 0-13-091977-2

Prentice-Hall International (UK) Limited, *London*
Prentice-Hall of Australia Pty. Limited, *Sydney*
Prentice-Hall Canada Inc., *Toronto*
Prentice-Hall Hispanoamericana, S.A., *Mexico*
Prentice-Hall of India Private Limited, *New Delhi*
Prentice-Hall of Japan, Inc., *Tokyo*
Simon & Schuster Asia Pte. Ltd., *Singapore*
Editora Prentice-Hall do Brasil, Ltda., *Rio de Janeiro*

CONTENTS

PREFACE

Whatever your situation and whatever the reason, you're no doubt thinking exactly like a lot of other people did when they started NT. Something like: "I already know how to copy files on eight different systems, and now I'll waste a week figuring it out on this one as well..." It seems like you waste a week, sometimes two, getting comfortable with any new operating system. During that time your productivity plummets as you absorb all the simple little things you already know how to do somewhere else.

That's where this book comes in. Its goal is to teach you how to use the Windows NT user interface in just a few hours. The entire user interface–from how to copy files, to how to customize the wallpaper, to how to print a screen dump–is detailed here and presented in a format that allows rapid learning. This book assumes you have work to get done, so it quickly points out everything needed to be productive.

This book also acts as a reference. For example, if you want to know how to copy a file from one directory to another, you can quickly find a concise answer that details the three different options available. When you get stuck, you can use this book to get un-stuck immediately.

You will find that each chapter (except the first one, which is a general introduction) covers a specific tool or program in NT. Every chapter starts with an Executive Summary of the tool. If you like, you can flip through the book and quickly read these summaries to see what all the different pieces do. Each chapter also contains a Guided Tour of the application so you can become familiar with its capabilities quickly while you learn your way around. The chapters also provide a list of common questions and answers, as well as detailed descriptions of all that's possible with each tool. Finally, the book contains an extensive and carefully structured index that helps you find needed information quickly whenever a problem arises.

Using this book as your guide, you should come up to speed on NT very quickly, and be ready to get useful work done in no time.

Who Needs this Book?

This book is designed primarily for people moving from other systems to Windows NT. It's meant to teach all the commonplace things you need to do every day, as quickly as possible. The book assumes you know what a file is and that you're familiar with a mouse, double-clicking, and so on. It does *not* assume you have experience with DOS or Microsoft Windows.

If you are new to workstation computing, or if you have never seen or used a mouse before, then a system like Windows NT can be frustrating initially. We have watched 50 and 60 year old managers pick up and use a mouse for the first time and we understand their predicament. Please see Appendix A. It summarizes all the fundamentals necessary to bootstrap yourself into this new environment as quickly as possible.

If you are an experienced Windows 3.1 user, then a lot of NT will already be familiar to you. There are some differences, however, particularly in the File Manager. All differences associated with the NT file system–security, extended file attributes, the network, etc.–are isolated in Chapter 5. Printing is also different and it's described in Chapter 6. See Chapters 12, 17, and 18 as well.

This book is not intended as a substitute for the documentation. Although it does contain quite a bit of material, it cannot contain everything. What the book will do, however, is point out all the things you'll need to use on a daily basis. You can then supplement the book's information with information from on-line Help files. In this way, you should have everything you'll ever need to use Windows NT. See Sections 1.5 and 7.5.3 for details on using the Help system and for information on the Command Line Help system.

Questions and Comments

If you use this book and find that you have questions, or if the book is missing something you needed, or if you have any suggestions or comments, we'd like to hear from you. You can reach us at the following address:

Interface Technologies
P.O. Box 841
Zebulon, NC 27597

See Appendix D for more information on reaching us via e-mail.

Where to Start

The following road map will help you decide how to get started with this book.

- If you have not yet installed Windows NT, then you need to install it. See Appendix B and the documentation that came with the system.
- If you have never used a mouse or a Graphical User Interface (GUI) before, you need to start by learning some basic skills. Turn to Appendix A.
- If you want to quickly get a feeling for what all the different pieces in Windows NT do, you can turn to the Executive Summaries at the beginning of each chapter. These summaries describe each tool in a few paragraphs and provide an overview of the entire system very quickly.
- If you want to jump in and start trying things out, turn to Chapter 1 and learn how to log in. Then run through the Guided Tours you'll find in every chapter. You can finish the Guided Tours in an hour or two and they should leave you completely familiar with the most useful parts of each component.
- If you need to add a new account or perform some other basic administrative task, see Appendix C. For more advanced administrative skills, see the third book in this series, *Windows NT Administration: Single Systems to Heterogeneous Networks.*
- The book is divided between system tools (such as the File Manager and Command Line) and applications (like the word processor and the calendar program) at Chapter 8. If you are more interested in applications you may wish to jump in at Chapter 8.

INTRODUCTION

Windows NT represents the high end of the Microsoft Windows family of operating system products. It offers all the features of a modern operating system such as UNIX, but its power is covered by the familiar (in the PC world) Windows user interface. This interface appears in one form or another on every product in the Windows family, and it's remarkably consistent from one end of the product line to the other.

This chapter introduces Windows NT. It offers a brief overview of the Microsoft Windows family and NT's position in that family. Also, it familiarizes you with the unique capabilities that NT has to offer. The chapter then shows how to log in, log out, and work with the Help system. Subsequent chapters discuss the different components that make up the user interface.

1.1 Road Map

- If you haven't installed NT yet, go to Appendix B.
- If you've never used a mouse before, go to Appendix A.
- If you want to log in and try out NT immediately, go to Section 1.3.
- If you want a brief introduction to the different tools available in Windows NT, read the Executive Summaries at the beginning of each chapter.
- If you want to learn a little about the history of Windows NT and the NT philosophy, read on.

1.2 A Brief History of Windows NT

Windows NT is a complete, modern operating system that uses the familiar Windows 3.1 graphical user interface (GUI) as its primary method of com-

1

munication with the user. In order to understand what all of that really means, it's helpful to look briefly at the history of Windows NT to place it in its proper historical context.

Currently, there are several familiar GUIs on the market: the Macintosh system from Apple Computer (the system that started the whole trend toward GUIs) running on Apple's proprietary hardware, the Windows family from Microsoft running on generic PC hardware, the Motif system running on high-end workstations under UNIX, OS/2 on PC hardware, the Next Step system, the Amiga, and so on. All these systems do generally the same thing in generally the same way, at least from a user's perspective. For example, a typical user could sit down on any of these systems and create a memo, paint a picture, or send e-mail without a lot of difficulty. Also, all the systems are moving closer to each other. Since they all seem to be borrowing or stealing features from each other as quickly as possible, they'll all function nearly alike eventually.

The Microsoft Windows family, by any financial measure, is the most successful of these systems. Since Windows will run on almost any PC-compatible hardware, it has been installed on millions of machines and is used by millions of people daily. Because of its success, Microsoft has released several different Windows products to appeal to specific sub-audiences among its throng of users.

The first product of the three is plain Windows, or "Windows 3.1." After several years of fits and starts, Microsoft finally got Windows "right" in version 3.1. Sales have been massive. Windows 3.1 is now the "entry level" product intended for single-user installations in the home or small business environment (see Figure 1.1).

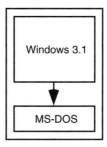

Figure 1.1
A single-user Windows 3.1 setup.

The intermediate product is "Windows for Workgroups." Windows for Workgroups looks just like Windows 3.1 to the user, but it contains extra programs and features that let it exploit local area networks. A Windows for Workgroups system can easily share directories, disks, and printers among several interconnected machines. The system also allows for personal intercommunication using e-mail and talk programs. It is therefore intended for small or intermediately sized groups of PCs typically seen in a small business or in an individual department of a larger company (see Figure 1.2).

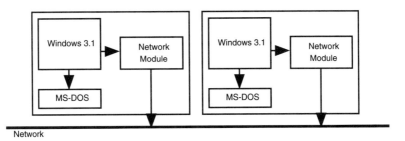

Figure 1.2
A multi-user Windows for Workgroups setup.

Windows 3.1 and Windows for Workgroups are built "on top" of MS-DOS, the Microsoft operating system for PC-class machines. This layering of systems is a liability because MS-DOS is primitive by today's standards. MS-DOS has a very simple file system with limited features and no security. MS-DOS offers none of the capabilities the user would expect to find in a "real" operating system–features such as virtual memory, multiple processes, and inter-process communication. Windows takes care of some of these problems itself as best it can. For example, it offers a good memory management system and cooperative multi-tasking. But, because it is built on DOS, the system is fragile and the file management facilities are poor. The system is also permanently attached to PC-compatible hardware. There is no easy way to move it to other platforms.

Windows NT, the third product in the Windows line, is Microsoft's answer to these problems. It is a complete, monolithic, modern operating system built from the ground up. There are no separate modules and no DOS (see Figure 1.3). It offers everything you would expect to find in a modern operating system, as shown in the list of capabilities below:

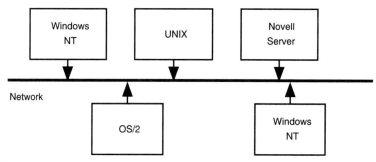

Figure 1.3
Windows NT on a heterogeneous network.

- 32-bit instructions and memory addressing
- Preemptive multi-tasking
- Multi-processing
- Multiple platforms (Intel, MIPS, Alpha, etc.)
- Threads
- Remote procedure calls
- Total network support (TCP/IP, NetBUI, etc.)
- Secure file system (C2 certified)

Windows NT contains a new, fully secure file system called the NT File System (NTFS). Windows NT is also built with portability in mind and it will run on a variety of platforms and CPU architectures and look exactly the same on each one. As you can see, NT's capabilities are patterned along the lines of an operating system like UNIX, and in several cases features such as RPCs were borrowed directly and completely from the UNIX world.

Microsoft has covered all the power in Windows NT with the familiar Windows 3.1 interface found in the other Windows products. This decision means that anyone familiar with previous versions of Windows can use NT right out of the box. Everything looks almost exactly the same. The only changes the user sees when comparing NT to the Windows for Workgroups interface are the security features in the File Manager (see Chapter 5) and the log on screen that insures these security features work.

1.3 The NT Philosophy

Every operating system has some sort of philosophy that drives its design and determines the audience it appeals to in the marketplace. For example, there is a very definite UNIX philosophy. The designers and creators of UNIX made the assumption that UNIX users are knowledgeable computer experts who know what they are doing. UNIX also generally assumes that hardware is community property meant to be shared. For example, many people can log in on one machine at the same time and share it. Everyone prints to a printer on a first come, first serve basis.

NT has a somewhat different philosophy. Quite a bit simpler to learn and use than UNIX, NT's command shell has far fewer commands and each command has far fewer options. Moreover, the graphical tools are all straightforward and intuitive.

NT also assumes that someone owns each piece of equipment. For example, if there is a workstation sitting on your desk then it is *your* workstation. Only one person can be logged in at a time. If there is a printer attached to the workstation, it's your printer. Someone else can use your printer, with your permission, but you have priority and there's nothing anyone can do about it.

The NT philosophy makes room for external administration. For example, if your machine is sitting on a network in a large company, an Administrator can enter your machine over the network to update software, change accounts, and so on. Presumably this administrative work takes place to make life on your machine better, in a manner similar to a repair person you might allow into your home. However, it's still your machine.

1.4 Getting Started with NT

You have to "log in" to your workstation before you can use Windows NT. If you've never worked with a system that requires users to log in, then this step may seem like a pain in the neck. However, it's really quite important.

You have a lock on your house because your house contains items that belong to you and are important to you. You don't want just anyone walking into your house and pawing through your belongings, so you lock it. You have friends and family whom you welcome into your home, so you give them a key to get in. Your computer is the same way. Its hard disk contains information that belongs to you and is important to you. You don't want people viewing that information without your permission. The log in screen guarantees that only those people who have permission to use your machine–only those with a key–get into your system.

If you followed the installation instructions in Appendix B, then your machine should have two *accounts*–an Administrator account and a user account for your general use. It is a good idea to save the administrative account for administrative purposes and use the user account for day-to-day work (See Appendix C for a discussion). If the machine was set up by someone else (e.g., by a network Administrator in your company) then the person who set it up probably created a user's account and told you the account name and password.

Turn on your machine and get NT up and running. A small dialog box appears asking you to press the Ctrl-Alt-Del key sequence to start. Find the Control Key, the Alt key, and the Delete key and press all three simultaneously. If you are new to Windows and DOS, this may seem like a very odd triplet. From the oldest IBM PC to the latest PC clone, this trio of keys has always meant "reset," and in a DOS machine it reboots the CPU. In NT, it's used at log in and log out as a way of guaranteeing that the log on window is authentic.

Now you see the "Welcome" dialog, as shown in Figure 1.4. If you never used a mouse before, or if you don't know how to use the elements you see in the log in window, or if you have problems with the directions, please turn to Appendix A at this point. This appendix will help you learn about the mouse, as well as other windowing vocabulary like "click," "drag," "button," "dialog," and so on. It also goes through the log in procedure in slow motion.

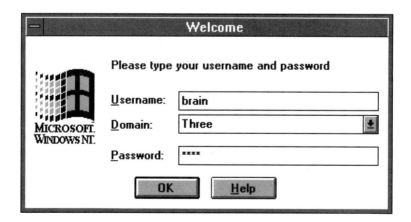

Figure 1.4

The Welcome dialog.

In the Welcome dialog box, type the user name for your user account into the top text area, the account's password into the password area, and click on OK. You can generally ignore the Domain field unless there are NT Advanced servers available on your network. If there are, the Domain field is used to choose one. Ask your administrator for assistance.

If your log in name or password is rejected, try again. If you continue to be rejected then see Appendix C or your administrator for help in creating or fixing your user account. As you are logging in you may see a dialog warning you that the system is unable to form a connection. This is not serious. It means that some drive or printer on the network cannot be found. Dismiss the dialog and continue. You will eventually see a screen that looks something like Figure 1.5. If not, look in the upper right corner of each window on the screen for a small down-pointing arrow (see Figure 1.6) and click on each one until you get to a screen that looks like Figure 1.5. The small down-pointing arrow is the *minimize button* and it's used to minimize, or iconify, an application. If the system beeps when you click on the arrow, look for a dialog box (a smaller window toward the center of the screen) and click the OK button to dismiss it.

1.5 Standard Window Features

The screen in Figure 1.5 is called the *desktop*. One or more applications are currently running on the desktop but they've been *minimized* into icons on the bottom of the screen. To use an application, you double-click on its icon. Right now, if you double-click on the Program Manager icon the *main application window* for the Program Manager will open.

Along the top of the Program Manager is the Title Bar. You can move the window itself by clicking on the Title Bar with the mouse and then dragging the window where you want it. If you double-click on the Title Bar the application will *maximize* itself (it will fill the entire screen). Double-click on the Title Bar again, or click on the double arrow in the upper right corner of the window. Either method will return the window to its original size.

You can re-size the window by moving the cursor along any outer edge of the window frame until it changes to a double arrow shape. The double arrow allows you to re-size the window by dragging. Try re-sizing the Program Manager window. You can make it any size you want.

Figure 1.5
The main screen.

Figure 1.6
The minimize button, found in the upper right corner of most windows.

1.6 The Help System

The on-line Help system provides a great deal of detailed information about Windows NT. You can therefore use it in conjunction with this book to look up details like obscure command line options in DOS commands. The Help system is uniform across all applications.

Along the top of the Program Manager window you see a bar containing the words "File," "Options," "Windows," and "Help." This is the *Menu Bar.* Different applications may have different Menu Bars, but all Menu Bars contain a *Help* menu. If you single-click on the word **Help,** a menu drops down displaying the different Help options. The Program Manager has a typical Help menu with four options:

1. Contents
2. Search On...
3. Help on Help
4. About Program Manager

The Help system is very easy to use. Click on the Contents item and the Program Manager will invoke Help. It comes up as a separate window displaying the *Contents screen* for the Program Manager's Help system. Read through this screen. Anywhere you see underlined green words (on a black and white monitor look for underlined words), you can single-click on those words to get more information. If you want to go back to the previous screen you were reading, you can click on the **Back** button near the top of the help window.

Near the **Back** button there's another button labeled **Search** or **Index.** This button produces a dialog containing key words for the Program Manager. If you select one of these key words and then click on the **Show Topics** button, different topics associated with that key word will appear in the lower list. Select one of the topics by double-clicking on it, or by single-clicking and pressing the **Go to** button.

Clear the Help system off your screen by minimizing it or by closing it. You close it in one of three ways:

1. Open the Help window's File menu and chose the Exit option.
2. Click on the small box in the upper left corner (if you want to use the keyboard, press Alt-space) and the *System menu* opens. This menu contains options pertaining to the window itself and is available in all applications. Choose the Close option.

3.   Double-click on the small box in the upper left corner of the Help window.

Go back to the Help menu of the Program Manager. One option reads "Help on Help." This Help screen describes the Help system itself. Read the screen to learn more about using on-line Help.

1.7 Logging Off

You want to be sure to log off of your account when finished because this action protects the security of the account. If you don't log off then anyone can come along and do whatever they want with your machine. There are two different ways to log off of a Windows NT workstation: You can log off so that someone can log in again later, or you can shut down so the machine can be turned off.

At the bottom of the File menu in the Program Manager you'll find a Log off and a Shutdown option. Choose one or the other and answer the dialog that appears. Alternately, you can press Ctrl-Alt-Del at any time. A dialog will appear that allows you to lock your screen temporarily, log off, shut down, or change your password (see Figure 1.7). Choose whichever option is appropriate.

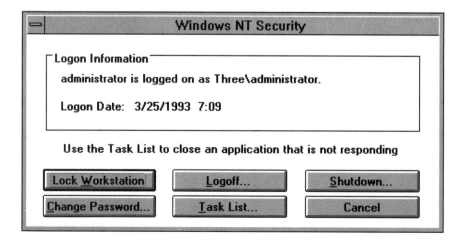

Figure 1.7
The Windows NT security dialog.

1.8 A Note About Passwords

Your password is an important piece of information. You want to keep it to yourself. You wouldn't leave your house keys lying around and the same applies to your password. Don't write it down and don't give it to other people. If others must use your computer, give them a separate account (see Appendix C).

When you select a password, make it fairly obscure. Do not use your first name, or your birthday, or your wife's birthday, or your favorite music groups. They're all too obvious, and someone who knows what they're doing will guess at them first. Do not make it a normal English word that someone can look up in the dictionary. It has become great sport on UNIX machines to crack passwords automatically by comparing encrypted dictionary words with the password database. Although the database in NT is not as wide open as it is in UNIX, if you simply add a digit somewhere in your password you solve that problem.

To change your password, log in to your account and press Ctrl-Alt-Del. When you see the dialog shown in Figure 1.7, click on the **Change Password** button and fill in the appropriate fields. The system makes you enter your new password twice to eliminate typos.

1.9 Conclusion

You now know how to log in to an NT workstation and how to use the Help system. That's all you need to get started. In the remainder of this book, each chapter covers a specific tool or application available in Windows NT. The chapters are arranged in a logical order but, if you want to jump around, feel free to do so and have fun. In the next chapter we discuss the Program Manager in detail, a good place to begin.

THE PROGRAM MANAGER

2

The Program Manager is normally the first thing you see when you log into a fresh installation of Windows NT. If the account you are using has been customized in some way, the Program Manager may be iconified or hidden by another window, but it's still there. If you are logged in, then the Program Manager is somewhere on the desktop.

The Program Manager is used to start other applications, and in this chapter you'll learn about its various capabilities.

2.1 Road Map

- If you don't know how to use a mouse, see Appendix A.
- If you haven't installed Windows NT yet, see Appendix B.
- If you haven't logged in yet, see Section 1.4 or Appendix A.
- If you want to begin using the Program Manager immediately, see the Guided Tour in section 2.3.
- If you need answers to common questions, see Section 2.4

2.2 Executive Summary

The Program Manager organizes all the different applications on your machine by collecting them in one place for easy access. The Windows user interface could have been designed without the Program Manager: For example, the Macintosh accomplishes about the same thing as the Program Manager using its equivalent of the File Manager (see Chapter 4). However, the Program

Manager is a convenience that makes it easy to use all the different applications available on your machine.

A typical Program Manager window is shown in Figure 2.1. It organizes your applications into *groups* that contain *icons* for each application. The groups themselves are represented by icons arranged along the bottom of the Program Manager window. Double-clicking on a group icon opens the group window containing the application icons for that group. To start the application you want, you double-click on its icon.

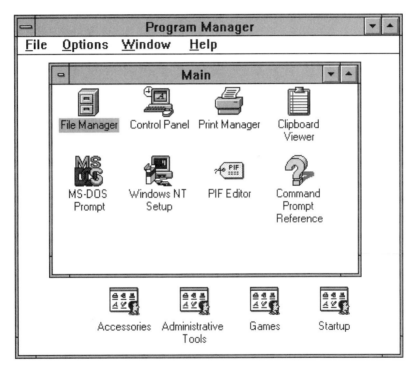

Figure 2.1
The Program Manager.

You can easily add new application groups to the Program Manager, and you can also copy or move icons among the different groups. An application icon can be copied into several groups so that it's conveniently available wherever it is needed. When a new application is installed, it's a simple matter to bring its icon into the Program Manager. Most programs do this for you automatically.

When you are ready to log off or shut down your system, use the **Logoff** and **Shutdown** options found in the File menu of the Program Manager, or press Ctrl-Alt-Del.

2.3 Guided Tour

The first thing to do is log in (see Section 1.4 or Appendix A if you haven't logged in yet).

Once you're logged in, the Program Manager should be the top window on your screen. If it's iconified, you can open it either by double-clicking on its icon or using the Alt-Tab key. Press and hold down the Alt key. Then press the tab key.

The Program Manager window may be filled with other small windows. These windows are called *group windows*. If any are open, like the "Main" group window in Figure 2.1, click on their minimize buttons (the small down-pointing arrow in the upper right hand corner) to turn them into icons. Minimize all open windows for now so that we're synchronized. Along the bottom of the Program Manager window you'll find a set of *group icons* (see Figure 2.1). A standard NT installation will have five:

- Main: Applications that are fundamental to the use of NT, such as the Control panel (Chapter 2), the File Manager (Chapter 3), and the Print Manager (Chapter 4).
- Accessories: Useful accessories like the Clock, Notepad, Calculator, and Paint program.
- Administration: Tools used to administer your system. Most of their capabilities are available only if you log in as the Administrator.
- Start-up: A special group. Any application icon contained in this group will start automatically whenever you log into this account.
- Games: A few games to entertain you.

Double-click on the different group icons so you can see the applications available in each. Each application is represented by an application icon.

You start an application from the Program Manager by double-clicking on its icon. Try this with the Notepad application, which is found in the Accessories group. Double-click on the Accessories icon and, when the Accessories window opens, double-click on the Notepad icon. Quit the Notepad application by choosing the **Quit** option in the File menu. Or you can minimize it or leave it running, and then bring the Program Manager back to the top by clicking on the Program Manager window or using the Alt-Tab keystroke. Start several other accessory programs to practice.

It is easy to create new groups and move or copy icons between different groups. A useful group to create is one that contains all the applications you use most frequently. By placing all their icons in one group, you make it easy to start these applications. To create a new group, use the **New** option in the File menu. Select the Personal Program Group item, and name the group "Common" (or something similar) in the dialog that follows. Now, copy several frequently used application icons to the new Common group. To copy the Control Panel icon, for example, take the following steps:

1.   Open the Main group.
2.   Click once on the Control Panel icon to select it.
3.   Then, Ctrl-click on the Control Panel icon and, while the mouse button and Control key are still down, drag it to the Common group. This is called Ctrl-dragging.
4.   Release the icon.

An alternative to the above is to use the **Copy** command in the File menu to copy the icons where you want them. You might try this with several other icons to familiarize yourself with the procedure.

When you have several icons in the new "Common" group, use the **Arrange Icons** option in the Window menu to align them in a uniform manner. The **Arrange Icons** option can also be used to arrange group icons in the same way (once all the group windows are closed).

If you wish to delete a group or application icon, you can select the icon you want by clicking on it and then choosing the **Delete** option in the File menu. Try this by creating a new group icon called "junk" and then deleting it again.

The Start-up group lets you select applications that start automatically when you log in. For example, if you copy the Clock icon into the Start-up group, it will start automatically every time you log in. Take the following steps:

1.   Open the Accessories group.
2.   Click on the Clock icon.
3.   Ctrl-drag the icon to the Start-up group.

4.   Check the Options menu and choose the **Save Settings Now** option, or make sure that **Save Settings on Exit** is turned on. If it is turned on, it will have a check mark next to it. If it is not, select it and then look at the menu again to see that the check mark is there.

5.   Log off and log back into the same account. The clock will start automatically.

6.   If you like, you can click on the Clock icon in the Start-up group and then select the **Properties** option in the File menu. Choose the **Start Iconified** option in the dialog by clicking on the small square. The Clock will now start iconified each time you log in. If it starts at normal size, it will remember its size and position from the last session as long as you have the **Save Settings On Exit** option enabled in the Options menu.

When you are ready to log off or shut down your system, use the **Logoff** and **Shutdown** options found in the File menu of the Program Manager, or press Ctrl-Alt-Del.

2.4 Common Questions

How do I start an application from the Program Manager?
Find the application in one of the Program Manager's groups. Double-click on the application's icon. As an alternative, you can single-click on the icon and then choose the **Open** option in the File menu. Or you can single-click the icon and then press the Enter key. It's also possible to select the **Run** option in the File menu and type the command line invocation for the command.

How do I create a new application icon?
How do I add a new application to the Program Manager?
If you install a new Windows NT application, it will generally install its icon in the Program Manager for you automatically. If not, see Section 2.6.1.1 for more information.

How do I create a new group?
Select the **New** option from the File menu and click on the **Personal Program Group** button.

How do I move and copy application icons among groups?
To move an icon from one group to another, simply drag it to the new

group. You can also use the **Move** option in the File menu. To copy an icon, click on it to select it. Then Ctrl-drag it to the new destination. The **Copy** option in the File menu can also be used.

How do I make programs automatically start whenever I log in?
Copy the program's icon into the Start-up group.

How do I change the icon on an application?
Click on the current icon to select it. Choose the **Properties** option in the File menu. Click on the **Change Icon** button. Most DLL and EXE files contain icons, so you might try looking around by changing the File Name field. A file that contains many icons is `progman.exe`.

How do I clean up the appearance of the icons? They are uneven and floating in the middle of the screen.
Choose the **Arrange Icons** option in the Window menu.

When I change things on the desktop and log out, the system forgets the new arrangement the next time I log in. Why?
You need to choose the **Save Settings on Exit** option in the Options menu.

I have tried using the Alt-Tab keys as suggested but they don't do anything. Why?
Turn on this capability in the **Desktop** applet of the Control Panel (see Chapter 3 for more information).

2.5 Tips

The Alt-Tab keys are a good way to get back to the Program Manager quickly from another application.

If you don't want the Program Manager cluttering up the screen after you've used it to start an application, select the **Minimize After Use** option in the Options menu.

The easiest way to add a new application icon is to drag the application's executable file icon (ending in .exe), or PIF file (ending in .pif), from the File Manager into a group in the Program Manager. If it is a Windows or Windows NT executable, it will pick up its icon automatically. If not, it will display a default icon. To change the default icon, use the **Properties** option in the File menu of the Program Manager to select a new icon.

❗ You can use the **Logoff** or **Shutdown** options in the File menu when you're ready to exit your account. A quicker way, however, is to hit Ctrl-Alt-Del and choose the **Logoff** or **Shutdown** buttons from there. This alternative lets you invoke a screen locking program as well.

2.6 Using the Program Manager

This section details all the different menu options available in the Program Manager.

2.6.1   The File Menu

This menu lets you create, move, and modify application and group icons.

2.6.1.1   The File | New Option

This option lets you create new groups or new application icons in the Program Manager's main window. When you select this option, you will first see a small dialog that lets you select either a group or an icon. (If you are logged on as the administrator, a third "common group" option is available.)

If you choose to create a group icon, you will see a second dialog. In this dialog type the name of the group as you want it to appear in the Program Manager's window.

If you choose to create an application icon, you will see a second dialog with four edit areas, as shown in Figure 2.2. The first is the Description field. It holds the name that will appear with the icon. The second field holds the Command Line invocation of the application. Click on the **Browse** button to browse through the executables. You can choose an executable file, a command file (ending in ".com"), or a PIF file. You can also place command line options into the Command Line field. For example, if you want a certain text file to start automatically in the Notepad application, you can say "notepad `sample.txt`" in this field and the file will be displayed when you click the icon. The Working Directory field lets you choose the starting directory for the application when it begins running. The Shortcut Key field lets you specify a Shortcut key that will activate the application from the Program Manager. Just move to that field and type the key that you want to use as a shortcut. It will appear automatically in that field.

Program Item Properties		
Description:	[ ]	OK
Command Line:	[ ]	Cancel
Working Directory:	[ ]	Browse...
Shortcut Key:	None	Change Icon...
☐ **Run Minimized**		Help

Figure 2.2
Creating a new program item.

What is a PIF file?
    You may have noticed an application called the PIF editor in the Main group, and in several places (e.g., the **Browse** button) that PIF files are recognized. PIF stands for Program Information File. These files allow a DOS program to interact with the Windows system in a friendly way. In the PIF editor you can specify how Windows should treat the DOS application. For example, you can specify the video and memory requirements, the display usage, and so on.
    Most DOS programs now ship with PIF files. You can also create your own by using the PIF editor and entering appropriate values into all the fields. You can then create an icon for the PIF file to run the DOS application, or double-click on the PIF file in the File Manager.

The system will display the application's icon, or a default icon, in the lower left portion of the dialog. Windows and Windows NT executables contain their icons within the executable itself. Non-windows applications place the icon either in an external file with a ".ico" extension, or place them in related ".dll" files. Try clicking on the **Change Icon** button and see what's available. You might try looking for some appropriate file names and typing them, along with their path, into the text field. For example, if you type a DLL file name and that file contains icons, you will see all the possibilities. The `progman.exe` file contains many icons and is a good choice when seeking new icons for your applications.

Another way to create items in the Program Manager is to drag an executable file from the File Manager into a group in the Program Manager. If an icon is available, it will be displayed automatically. See Chapter 4 for details on the File Manager.

There is also a **Run Minimized** check box in this dialog. If you click it, the application opens as an icon at the bottom of the desktop rather than a main window. This is especially handy with applications placed in the Start-up group.

2.6.1.2   The File | Open Option

This option is the same as double-clicking on a group or application icon. Select an icon and then choose this option. If it's an application icon, that application starts. If it's a group icon, the group's window opens.

2.6.1.3   The File | Move Option

This option lets you move an application icon from one group to another. It is the same as dragging the icon to the new group.

2.6.1.4   The File | Copy Option

This option lets you copy an application icon to a new group. It's the same as Ctrl-dragging an application icon to a new group.

2.6.1.5   The File | Delete Option

This option deletes an application icon or a group, along with all the icons it contains. Select the application or group by clicking on it. then choose **Delete** from the File menu or press the Delete key.

2.6.1.6   The File | Properties Option

This option displays the same dialog that appeared when the application icon was created (see Section 2.6.1.1). First click on an application to select it, then choose the **Properties** option. You can change the name of the icon, the application it invokes, the default directory, the Shortcut key, or the icon itself. See Section 2.6.1.1 for details.

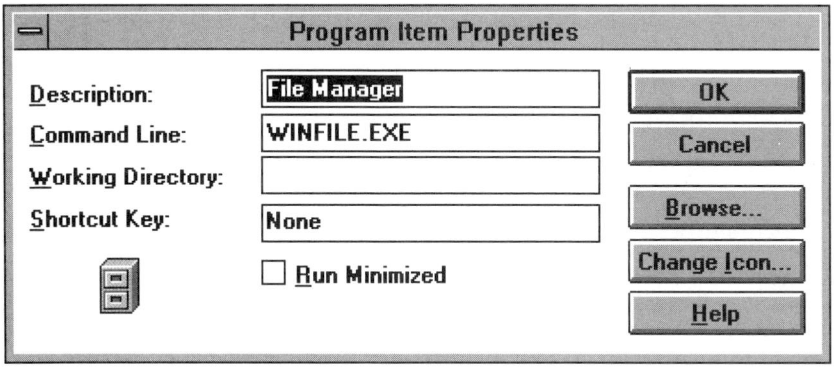

Figure 2.3
The Properties dialog.

2.6.1.7   The File | Run Option

This option lets you run an application as though you were invoking it from the command line. When you choose this option, you will see a dialog that lets you type in a command or browse through the available executables in the same way you browse in the Properties dialog.

2.6.1.8   The File | Logoff Option

This option lets you log out of your account so someone else can log in. You will be asked to confirm the action before you can log out.

2.6.1.9   The File | Shutdown Option

This option shuts down the entire system. A dialog will ask whether you want to restart the system after shutdown. After you shutdown, a dialog appears informing you that it's safe to turn the power off.

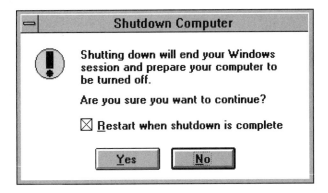

Figure 2.4
The Shutdown dialog.

2.6.2   The Options Menu

This menu lets you set options that control the behavior of the Program Manager. Clicking on these options toggles them on and off.

2.6.2.1   The Options | Auto Arrange Option

When the **Auto Arrange** option in the Options menu is on (it has a check mark next to it when it's on), icons are automatically aligned whenever they are moved or copied.

2.6.2.2   The Options | Minimize On Use Option

This option causes the Program Manager to iconify itself after an application is launched. This can help reduce screen clutter.

2.6.2.3   The Options | Save Setting On Exit Option

This option causes the NT system to save the arrangement of the Program Manager when you log off. It remembers which group windows are open, where windows in the Program Manager are located, and any new groups or icons that you created.

2.6.2.4   The Options | Save Settings Now Option

This option saves the current arrangement of the Program Manager to disk. It remembers which group windows are open, where windows in the Program Manager are located, and any new groups or icons that you created.

2.6.3   The Window Menu

This menu provides a list of the group icons. It also helps to arrange the windows on screen.

2.6.3.1   The Window | Cascade Option

This option neatly stacks the Program Manager's windows.

2.6.3.2   The Window | Tile Option

This option neatly tiles the Program Manager's windows.

2.6.3.3   The Window | Arrange Icons Option

This option neatly arranges all the icons along the bottom of the Program Manager and group windows.

THE CONTROL PANEL

3

The Control Panel lets you customize your account to match your personal style. You can change screen colors, customize fonts, personalize your desktop, tune the behavior of your keyboard and mouse, and control many other aspects of your account from the Control Panel.

3.1 Executive Summary

You use the Control Panel to personalize your account. Figure 3.1 shows what the Control Panel's main screen looks like. You activate its different functions by double-clicking on the icons or by selecting the item you want from the Settings menu. Four things you commonly do in the Control Panel are:

1. Change your display colors
2. Tune the feel of your keyboard and mouse
3. Customize the desktop
4. Modify the different fonts available in applications

There are many more features built into the Control Panel, but they're generally restricted to the Administrator (see Appendix C for a description of these options).

You'll most likely use the Control Panel after installing NT, or after getting your account, to match the system's behavior to your way of doing things. Later, you'll find yourself fine tuning the system as the mood strikes you.

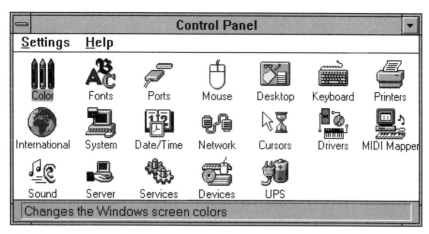

Figure 3.1
The Control Panel.

3.2 Guided Tour

Open the Control Panel by double-clicking on the Main group icon in the Program Manager and then double-clicking on the Control Panel icon. You will see a window filled with icons similar to the window shown in Figure 3.1. Each of these icons holds an *applet* that allows you to customize different aspects of the system.

One of the first things most people modify is the screen colors. If you double-click on the **Colors** icon, you'll see a dialog that lets you choose from a list of pre-packaged color schemes, as shown in Figure 3.2. Use the combo box (the box labeled "Color Schemes") to view the different schemes available. You can activate the combo box by clicking on the arrow, as shown in Figure 3.2. If you cannot find a scheme to your liking, you can build your own custom color scheme by clicking on the **Color Palette** button. The Color Palette provides specific color choices for each element in the desktop. Use the Color Palette's combo box to designate the element you want to change, then pick a new color from the palette. You can save the new color scheme under its own name.

The Control Panel's **Fonts** icon lets you add and remove fonts (see Figure 3.3). If you purchased a new True Type font, or some other type of font, you can add it to the font library on your hard disk by pressing the **Add** button. You can activate True Type fonts and make them the only fonts available in your applications by clicking the True Type button and then clicking on the check boxes that appear.

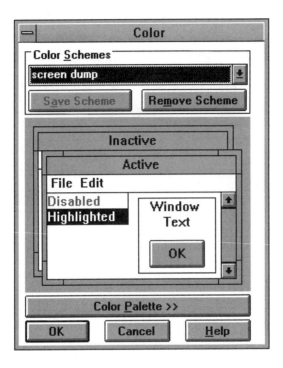

Figure 3.2
Picking a color scheme.

The **Mouse** and **Keyboard** icons let you customize the behavior of your mouse and keyboard (see Figures 3.4 and 3.5). If you click on the **Mouse** icon, you'll see a dialog that lets you control the mouse's tracking speed and its double-clicking speed. It also lets you swap mouse buttons if you're left-handed. The **Keyboard** icon lets you control the auto repeat speed for the keyboard and the amount of time that elapses before auto repeat begins.

The **Desktop** icon lets you change the appearance and behavior of your desktop (see Figure 3.6). For example, toward the bottom of the dialog is a Wallpaper section. Select a wallpaper file using the combo box, then choose between the Center and Tile options. If you choose **Center,** the wallpaper image will be centered on the screen. If you choose **Tile** it will be repeated across the screen as many times as its size permits. You can also invoke a screen saver here by choosing from the available screen savers and picking the delay time–the screen saver will be activated after that many minutes of inactivity. Other op-

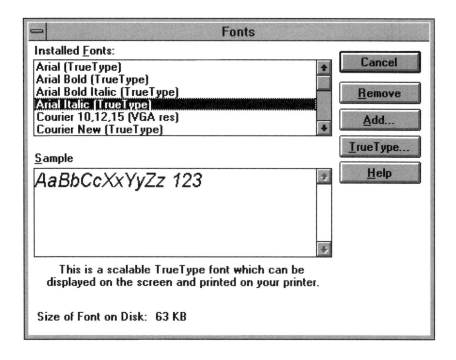

Figure 3.3
The Fonts applet.

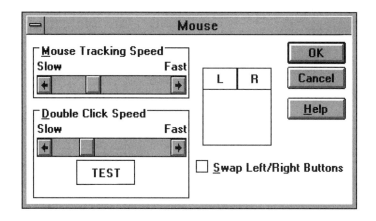

Figure 3.4
The Mouse applet.

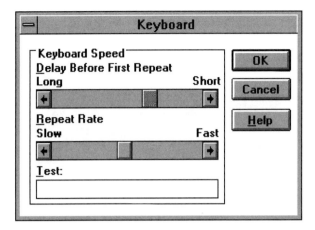

Figure 3.5
The Keyboard applet.

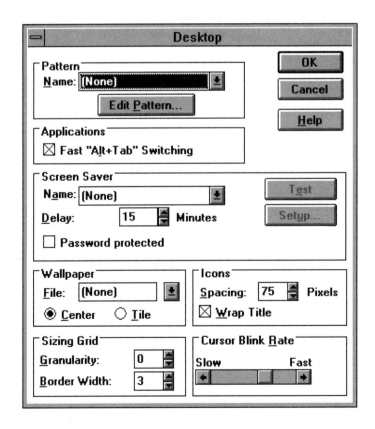

Figure 3.6
The Desktop applet.

tions include Patterns (which resemble wallpaper but are created by duplicating a small bitmap across the screen many times), icon spacing, and the sizing granularity. Try out these different options and see how they look on the desktop.

The Cursors icon lets you change and customize the cursor. Many people find animated cursors to be distracting, but others love them. Play with the different options and see how you feel.

If your system has the proper drivers and equipment installed, you can use the **Sound** icon to control the sounds that are generated by different error and alert states in the system. In the Sound dialog you choose the error state and the sound that should be generated (see Figure 3.7).

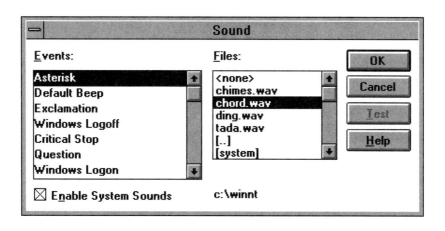

Figure 3.7
The Sound applet.

The **Ports** icon lets you change the settings of the communications ports you're using. This is important if you want to connect a modem to your system (see the Terminal application in Chapter 11). The **International** icon lets you set country-specific information such as the language and date format (see the KEYB command in Chapter 7). The **Date/Time** and **Time Zone** icons let you change the time and the way the system interprets it (see also the DATE and TIME commands in Chapter 7). You may or may not have permission to change these items, depending on how your account is set up.

Many of the icons in the Control Panel are applicable only to the Administrator. You may want to log off and switch over to the Administrator account to try some out (see Appendix C for more information). For example, a normal user cannot set the time and date; only the Administrator, or a "Power User," can.

3.3 Common Questions

How do I change my screen colors?
Double-click on the **Colors** icon.

I have looked at the available fonts in the Font applet, but none are available in my applications no matter what I do. Why?
If the printer is set to some sort of generic or low-functionality printer, many of the standard fonts will not show up in applications because the printer cannot support them (see Chapter 6 for details on the Print Manager).

How can I produce different sounds with my machine?
Use the **Sound** icon to customize the sound effects produced by error messages and certain special events such as logging on. Your machine must have a sound board and properly installed drivers for these changes to have any effect (in some cases, just the proper sound driver is required.

How do I change the background on my desktop?
How can I create my own wallpaper or use bitmaps I've downloaded as my wallpaper?
You change your wallpaper by double-clicking the **Desktop** icon and choosing from among the available bitmaps. You can create your own bitmaps with the Paintbrush application (see Chapter 9), or you can download a virtually infinite supply of bitmaps from BBSs. These custom bitmap files must be copied into the directory that Windows NT searches for bitmaps, generally the `winnt` or windows directory. The easiest way to do this is to first look at some of the file names in the Wallpaper selection list, then use the File Manager (Chapter 4) to find one of those files. Next, load your custom bitmaps into that same directory and then choose the **Desktop** icon again. Your new bitmaps should now appear in the Wallpaper selection list. If it is a small bitmap, be sure to choose the Tile option when you select it or you won't be able to see it.

How do I change my screen resolution?
See Appendix C.

I'm left-handed. Is there a way to make the mouse work in a left-handed way?
Use the **Mouse** icon to change mouse buttons.

Where can I go to get other fonts?
Generally you can download new fonts from BBSs, or companies like Microsoft and Bitstream will sell you font packages. Install the new fonts with the **Fonts** icon.

Where can I get other sounds for the sound applet?
BBSs are littered with WAV files (files ending in a ".wav" extension) that you can use. Or, if your sound board supports it and you have a microphone, you can record your own sounds. Use the Sound Recorder application in the Accessories group of the Program Manager.

Why am I unable to use some of the applets? I get "Access Denied" or "Insufficient Privilege" warnings when I try them.
You need to have administration privileges to use many of the applets (see Appendix C).

I have a high resolution screen and I can barely see the window borders. How do I make the borders wider so re-sizing is easier?
Use the **Border Width** field in the **Desktop** icon.

3.4 Details

This section briefly describes the purpose of each of the standard applets. You'll find that most are very easy to use and that the on-line Help system describes them in detail if you have problems. Press the Help button in each applet for details.

3.4.1 Color

This icon lets you change the colors used for the desktop and its windows. You can choose from standard color schemes (anything from the default colors to "Hot Dog Stand"), or create your own custom color schemes. In a custom color scheme you can choose the color for each element on the desktop–window borders, menu bars, title bars, and so on (see the Guided Tour in Section 3.2 for details).

3.4.2   Fonts

The **Fonts** icon lets you add and remove fonts from the system. For example, if you purchased or downloaded new fonts, the Fonts dialog will let you install them. Using the **True Type** button lets you change the system's behavior toward True Type fonts.

3.4.3   Ports

This icon lets you set the baud rate, data bits, parity, and so on of the available communications ports in your machine. Select the port you want to change and then adjust the appropriate setting for it in the Settings dialog.

3.4.4   Mouse

The **Mouse** icon lets you change the tracking speed, double-click speed, and the button orientation of the mouse. Left-handed users can switch mouse buttons in this dialog.

3.4.5   Desktop

The **Desktop** icon lets you change the wallpaper or pattern displayed as the Desktop's background. It also lets you enable the Alt-Tab keys and the Screen Saver option. Other adjustments include the icon spacing on the desktop, the cursor blink rate, and the border size of windows.

3.4.6   Keyboard

This icon lets you adjust the auto repeat rate of your keyboard.

3.4.7   International

In this icon you can adjust the language used by the system, the keyboard layout, the standard units for measurements, and the list separator–along with the date, time, currency, and number formats used within applications.

3.4.8   System

The **System** icon lets you set environment variables used in your account (see Chapter 7 for details). If you are the Administrator, you can also adjust the size and location of the virtual memory file (see Appendix C).

3.4.9   Date/Time

The **Date/Time** icon lets you adjust the system date and time. You must be an Administrator or Power User to use this icon (see Appendix C).

3.4.10   Networks

This icon lets you add new network drivers following installation of a new network card. This is an administrative task.

3.4.11   Drivers

The **Drivers** icon lets you add and remove device drivers for equipment such as sound cards, MIDI devices, and CD drives. This is an administrative task.

3.4.12   Time Zone

This icon lets you change the system's time zone and daylight savings time behavior.

3.4.13   MIDI Mapper

The **MIDI Mapper** icon lets you change the system's MIDI setups.

3.4.14   Sound

The **Sound** icon lets you change the sounds associated with different system errors and warnings, as well as log on and log off sounds (see question 3 in Section 3.2).

3.4.15   Server

The **Server** icon shows you statistics about your machine's performance as a server. For example, it shows how many sessions are connected to your machine, how many files other users currently have open, and so on (see Chapter 5 for details on setting up network connections).

3.4.16   Services

This icon shows the current state of the different services available on your machine. If you are the Administrator, you can start and stop different services.

3.4.17   UPS

The **UPS** icon lets you manage your connection to an uninterruptable power supply. This is an administrative task.

THE FILE MANAGER—BASICS

4

The File Manager is the application used most often when working with the Windows NT user interface. It lets you manage all the files you can access, both on your local machine and over the network–copy them, move them from place to place, delete and rename them, and so on. In this chapter we discuss the basics, those normal things you do with files on a day-to-day basis. In the next chapter we discuss network aspects of the File Manager and all the different security options available in the NT file system.

4.1 Road Map

- If you are unfamiliar with the way files are traditionally managed on PC systems, please read Section 4.2 first.
- If you understand the normal way PCs handle files but are unfamiliar with the NT file system and plan on using it, then read Section 4.3.
- If you already use Windows 3.1 on a daily basis, go to Chapter 5.

4.2 PC-based File Systems

NT as shipped supports three different file systems:

1. The NT file system, which is preferred.
2. The MS-DOS file system, generally known as the File Allocation Table (FAT) file system.
3. The OS/2 High Performance File System (HPFS).

When NT was installed on your machine, either you or the Administrator decided which file system to use on the hard disk. However, you're likely to en-

35

counter other file systems, depending on where your network connects. And even if the NT file system is installed on your system, you still need to understand the FAT system because it's used on floppy disks, removable hard disks, CD-ROMs, and so on.

FAT is used whenever NT needs to work with transportable media. It's also used on millions of MS-DOS computers around the world. Primitive by modern standards, FAT has the advantage of ubiquity. If you've never used a PC, then you need to learn about the FAT system and the way a PC treats its disk drives in general, to feel comfortable in an NT environment.

If you call up a mail order company and order a typical MS-DOS or Windows PC for home use, it's going to arrive with three drives: an "A" drive that is a 1.2 Meg 5.25 inch floppy disk drive, a "B" drive that is a 1.44 Meg 3.5 inch floppy disk drive, and a "C" drive that is a hard disk of some capacity between 20 Meg and a Gig. You can *partition* the hard disk into multiple logical drives if you choose. You can also add other drives. For example, you might add a second hard disk, and it will be called "D." If you add a CD-ROM drive it will typically be called "E."

As you can see, each drive (or in some cases each partition on a drive) has its own *drive letter*. This naming system dates back to the old 8-bit CP/M days in the seventies and has been preserved in NT. If you're coming from a system like UNIX, where the file system is thought of as a single homogeneous directory tree, the drive letter concept is a different way to think about things. Drive letters are followed by a colon. For example, the statement "C:" on the command line means "default to drive C." See Chapter 7 for details.

The floppy disks on your NT machine support the FAT file system. Your CD-ROM drive, if you have one, is probably the same. The hard disk on your system may or may not be a FAT hard disk. It might have been formatted as an NT file system disk during the installation of NT. When you connect to drives over the net, you will find that they may be FAT, NT, or HPFS.

The FAT file system is easy to understand because it's so primitive. It supports a hierarchical (tree structured) file system similar to UNIX's, but just different enough to be incredibly annoying to former UNIX people (e.g., DOS uses a backslash instead of a slash as a separator, and case does not matter in DOS). A FAT file system has a root directory on each drive, known on the C drive, for example, as "C:\" (pronounced "C colon backslash"). Sub-directory names are separated by backslashes. The root directory can contain files and zero or more sub-directories.

Hierarchical file systems (also known as tree-structured file systems) are a fairly standard way to organize files. If you've never seen one before, here are the basics:

A hierarchical file system has what's known as a root directory. In NT the root is known as "C:\" on the C drive, "D:\" on the D drive, and so on. The backslash character is the name of the root directory. It can contain files and, if that's all it contains, then it's a flat file system. Each file might contain a document, a spreadsheet, a drawing, or whatever. However, the root directory can also contain *other directories,* which are named sections on the disk that hold files and still more directories. The Macintosh operating system popularized the concept of sub-directories as file folders. As a real file folder can contain documents, receipts, drawings, letters, etc., a directory can contain computer files that hold those same objects.

The directories form a tree. That is, they start at the root and can be thought of to branch out, diagrammatically, like an upside down tree (see Figure 4.1). The File Manager displays them a little differently to save screen space, as shown in Figure 4.2. Directories higher up in the tree are called *parents,* while the directories they contain are called their *children.*

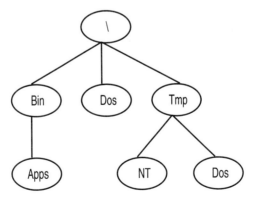

Figure 4.1
A tree structured directory.

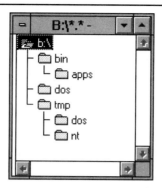

Figure 4.2
The File Manager representation of the same tree.

Figures 4.1 and 4.2 show only the directories. Each directory can also contain files.

The names of the set of directories that lead to a specific file are known as a *path*. For example, assume that the Apps directory in Figure 4.1 contains a file named `paper.txt`. The path to that file is `c:\bin\apps\paper.txt`. This naming scheme will be important when using DOS commands in Chapter 7 because that's the only way to talk about files. In the File Manager you'll see paths used in quite a few places because they are compact, and because Windows users are used to seeing things expressed that way. For example, the Copy dialog accepts a path name to indicate the place and name to copy.

There are two special file names used to work with the directory tree. The file name ".." (two dots) means, "the parent of the current directory." To talk about the directory `c:\bin\apps\..` is the same as talking about `c:\bin`. You'll see ".." in the File Manager. Double-clicking it simply means "go up one directory." The "." (one dot) file name represents the current directory.

On any given drive you're always "in" a specific directory. That directory is normally called the *default directory*, or the *current directory* for that drive. Each drive has its own default directory.

On a network, you can also use "UNC names: to talk about files on other machines. For example, **\\five\c\bin\samp.txt** talks about a file named samp.text in directory bin on drive C of a machine on the network named five. The double backslash denotes the machine name.

In the FAT file system, there is no security of any kind. If you can see the drive you can view any file on it. The file names are constrained by what's known as the eight-dot-three naming convention. That is, any file name must have no more than eight characters followed by a period followed by no more than three letters. The period and the three character extension are optional. A file name can contain letters or numbers and a few punctuation characters such as underscores, dashes, and dollar signs. Case does not matter in DOS–upper and lower case characters are identical. For example, the following file names are valid:

backit.bat

123.exe

report.txt

files.zip

a.lg

hello.doc

makefile

3-93_rpt.txt

By convention, the three character portion following the dot is called an *extension* and is used to indicate the file type. The following list identifies the most common extensions:

EXE   executable

COM   executable

TXT   text

BAT   DOS batch file

DLL   dynamic link library

HLP   help file

BMP   bitmap file

WAV   digitized sound file

TMP   temporary file

ZIP   Zip file, a common PC file compression and archiving format

You should stick to these conventions religiously when naming your files.

As in UNIX, the file name ".." means "the parent directory of this directory," and "." means "this directory." See the sidebar on tree structured directories if you are unfamiliar with the naming scheme. On networks, a double backslash at the beginning of the file name denotes a machine name, so **\\five\c\samp.txt** denotes the file samp.txt on the root directory of drive C on machine five.

There are four attribute bits associated with each file in a FAT file system:

Read only   File can be read but not modified or deleted.

Hidden   File name does not appear in normal directory listings.

System   File is used by the operating system.

Archive   File has been modified since the last back up.

You can set or un-set these bits at any time. See Section 4.8.1.6.

4.3 The NT File System

The NT file system is a modern file system. Like DOS, it uses the letter-based naming convention for each drive attached to the workstation. It's also a hierarchical file system that uses backslashes to separate sub-directories, as in DOS.

File and directory names in the NT file system can be as long as you like. The system also creates and exports an eight-dot-three version of each file name so that activities such as file copying to a FAT device, or directory browsing on a DOS-based machine connected to an NT drive over the network, work properly.

The NT file system also supports file security. NT itself places a layer of security on everything it controls. For example, if you share a FAT disk or directory on the network, you can protect it to allow access only to specific groups and individuals. On a disk formatted with the NT file system, however, you have much more control. You can specify that a directory, or even an individual file, can or cannot be read by a certain individual or group of people. The details are discussed in Chapter 5.

By using the NT file system you not only gain such things as long file names, but you also insure that your files are secure. If you have not given permission to see your files, then no one can get to them.

4.4 Executive Summary

The File Manager handles all the mundane file manipulation tasks. For example, it lets you copy files, move files, delete and rename files, change file properties (Read only, Hidden, etc.), search for files by file name, and so on. It's also in charge of sharing information over the network and managing file security. The latter two topics are discussed in the next chapter.

Figure 4.3 shows a typical File Manager screen. As you can see, the system can display the directory structure of a disk as well as the files inside of one directory. In addition, the File Manager lets you look at more than one drive at a time in separate windows.

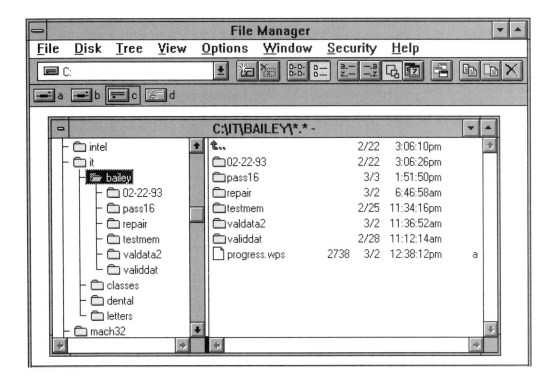

Figure 4.3
A typical File Manager screen.

The File Manager gives you a great deal of control over how files are viewed. For example, you can display just the file names so more files fit on screen, or you can select extra information, such as file size and creation date, to be displayed alongside each name. You can also sort the names in a variety of ways.

The File Manager supports several tools that make file manipulations easier. For example, you can search a disk for certain file names. You can also associate certain file extensions with specific applications and, by doing so, run applications directly from the File Manager very easily. This facility makes it extremely easy to browse through files in the File Manager and run them under their appropriate applications.

4.5 Guided Tour

Open up the File Manager from the Program Manager by double-clicking on the File Manager icon found in the Main group. As an alternative, you can put the File Manager into the Program Manager's Start-up group so it's always available on the desktop (see Section 2.2).

Start off by making sure that the current directory window is showing both the directory tree and the contents of a directory, as shown in Figure 4.4. If it isn't, open the **View** menu and select the **Tree and Directory** option. Notice that there is a thick black bar between the two horizontal scroll bars at the bottom of the window. You can drag this bar to change the amount of space devoted to the two sides of the window.

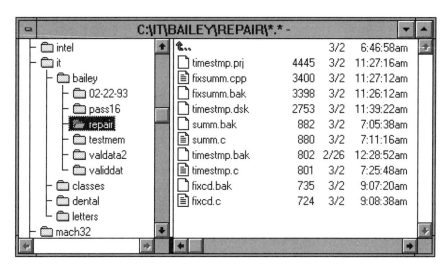

Figure 4.4
The tree and directory view.

Move the left-hand vertical scroll bar to the top (in the Tree and Directory view there are two horizontal and two vertical scroll bars). You will see the root directory and its sub-directories below it in the left window. Single-click on one of the directories. Its files appear on the right-hand side of the window, and several statistics will be printed in the status area at the bottom of the File Manager window. Click on a different directory and the files change accordingly.

If you double-click on a directory in the left side window, and if the directory contains sub-directories, the sub-directories will show up in the left-hand window. This is called *expanding* the branch. If you select the **Indicate Expandable Branches** option in the View menu, then the directories that contain other sub-directories will display plus signs so you know whether they can be expanded or not. Double-clicking on an expanded branch in the left side of the window will cause it to collapse again.

On the right side of the window you can work with individual files. Try some of the different options in the View menu. For example, try the **Name**, **All File Details**, and **Partial Details** options. The **Name** option shows just the file names so that many file names can fit on the screen at once. **All File Details** shows all details such as the creation date and time, file size, and attribute bits. **Partial File Details** lets you choose the details you want to see. Also try the different sorting options. The **By File Type** option lets you determine which types of files are displayed in the right-hand side of the window. For example, if you want hidden files displayed, or if you want to eliminate all directories from the right side of the window, you specify it here.

Single-click on one of the files in the window's right-hand side. It will highlight itself to show it's selected. It is also possible to Shift-click on files to select a group of files. To try this out, single-click on any file so that a single file is selected. Then hold down the Shift key and single-click on a different file. Every file between the first file and the Shift-clicked file will be selected. You can Ctrl-click a file to add it to or delete it from the group individually. Hold down the Ctrl key and click on any file. If that file is already in the current group it will be removed. If it's not in the group, it will be added.

Another way to select groups of files is to use the **Select** option in the File menu. The string "*.*" selects all files in the current directory. The string "*.txt" selects all TXT files in the directory. See below for a description of the two wild card characters used by NT.

Click on the root directory (the topmost entry in the left-hand side of the window) and then go to the File menu and select the **Create Directory** option. A dialog appears asking for the new directory name. Enter temp1 and the new directory will be created. If there are many directories on this disk you may have to scroll down to see the new entry, but it's there. Now create a second directory called temp2.

Use the View menu and select **All File Details** to ensure that you can see file sizes in the right side of the window. Click through several directories on the disk and find one that contains five or six relatively small files (the file size in bytes is right next to the name). Copy the files to `temp1`. To do this, select the files either one at a time or in a group, and then choose the **Copy** option in the File menu. In the dialog, indicate that you want them copied to the `\temp1` directory and click the OK button (or press return). Double-click on the `temp1` directory to make sure the files were copied.

Now move the files in `\temp1` to `\temp2`. You can use the same technique used in the previous paragraph. Select all the files and then select the **Move** option in the File menu, specifying `\temp2` as the destination. Or, you can select the files and then drag them to `\temp2`. When released in `\temp2`, the files will be moved to the new directory. It's obviously much quicker to use the drag technique to move files than the dialog technique.

The Copy dialog has a similar accelerator. To copy the files from `\temp2` to `\temp1`, select them and then hold down the Control key while dragging them to the new directory. When you drop the file at its destination, *be sure to release the mouse button and then the control key.* You have to use a little caution with this technique. If the Control key timing isn't just right, the files are moved rather than copied. Be sure to select the files first, and *then* Ctrl-drag them.

You move and copy directory trees using the same techniques. Just drag or Ctrl-drag one directory (from the tree side of the window) or a whole group of directories (from the directory side of the window) and place them where they belong. The entire directory tree of each selected directory will be copied.

All this time you've probably been getting messages like, "Are you sure you wish to move such and such a file?" If you tire of them, use the **Confirmation** item in the Options menu and indicate which operations you do and do not wish to be prompted on.

If you want to copy files from one drive to another (you cannot move files from drive to drive unless you use the Move dialog), you can do one of three things:

1. Use the Copy dialog from the **File | Copy** menu option and specify the destination drive and directory.
2. Open two windows in the File Manager simultaneously–one for each drive–and drag the files from one window to another. To open a second window, double-click on one of the drive icons near the Menu bar.

3.   Drag the files from the source directory and drop them onto one of the drive icons near the Menu bar. The files will be placed in the default directory on the second drive. The default directory is whichever directory is currently selected when you open a window for the second drive.

You can copy entire directory trees using the same techniques. Simply drag one or more file icons.

To delete files or whole directories, select the file(s) or directory(s) and press the Delete key or select the **File | Delete** option. Confirm that you wish to delete the files and they'll be permanently deleted.

To rename a file, select the file and choose the **File | Rename** option. Type the new name in the second text area (your first instinct will be to modify the file name in the upper text area, but this doesn't work), press OK, and the file will be renamed and appropriately re-sorted. Try renaming and deleting several of the files in your `temp1` and `temp2` directories.

The File menu contains a **Search** option that you can use to scan an entire drive or specific directories for files. For example, if you are looking for a file named `report3.txt` you can choose the **Search** option to locate it. First, click on the directory where you want the search to begin. Searching will occur in that directory and all its sub-directories so, if you select the root directory for the starting point, it will search the entire drive. Next, select the **File | Search** option and then enter the file name you seek. You can enter the exact file name if you know it, or you can use wild cards. For example, the string `*.txt` will search for all files with a TXT extension, or `report?.txt` will find all files that contain any single character following the word "report." These are not regular expressions in the UNIX sense. For example, you cannot search for `*x*.*i` as you can in UNIX. Generally, you can use one star before the period and one star after it, and it cannot precede other characters. You can use the "?" character anywhere except in place of the period. When the search finishes, the File Manager will display a separate window containing all the files that matched the search string. You can move, copy, or open the files in this window in the same way you would in any other window.

One of the handiest features in the File menu is the **Associate** option. You can associate files having specific extensions with specific applications. For example, you can form an association between TXT files and the Notepad application. You might also form an association between a bitmap file and the Paint program. To try out the **Associate** option, find a TXT file either by hunting around or by using the **Search** option. Click on it to select it. If its icon is hollow, that means no association has yet been formed with TXT files. On the other hand, if it contains several small horizontal lines it has an association. Double-click on it to view the file.

To create an association, click on a TXT file. Choose the **File | Associate** option. In the dialog box that appears select the Notepad application from the list and press OK. Now, when you double-click on any file having a TXT extension, the file will automatically open in Notepad. You can form other associations as you see fit. The list box in the **Associate** dialog offers suggestions for extensions to associate with each of the applications it's aware of. The **Open** option in the File menu can also be used to execute an associated application.

The Disk menu is used to manipulate disks and diskettes. You can use it to format diskettes, change their volume labels, and copy from one disk to another. For example, find a blank disk and stick it into the appropriate disk drive. Select the **Disk | Format** option. The dialog lets you choose the drive to format as well as the density. You can also choose the quick format option. If the disk has been formatted previously, the system can quickly re-format it by replacing the existing FAT with a blank one.

Most likely your File Manager is displaying a *Toolbar*. Look at the **Toolbar** option in the Options menu to see if it's checked. The Toolbar contains small buttons for several common menu options and it's useful because it accelerates your access to these options. Each button has the unique feature of not making sense until you've used it a few times. Then it makes a lot of sense. Figure 4.5 shows the Toolbar displayed by the **File Manager**. From left to right, the icons represent the following menu options.

Disk | Connect Network Drive
Disk | Disconnect Network Drive
View | Name
View | All File Details
View | Sort by Name
View | Sort by Type
View | Sort by Size
View | Sort by Date
Window | New Window

File | Copy

File | Move

File | Delete

Disk | Share As

Disk | Stop Sharing

Security | Permissions

Figure 4.5
The File Manager Toolbar.

4.6 Common Questions

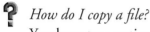 *How do I copy a file?*
You have two options:
A) Select a file and use the Copy dialog from the **File | Copy** menu
option to specify the destination drive and/or directory.
B) Select a file and then Ctrl-drag it to the new sub-directory or drive. If
you have two windows open you can copy between the two windows.

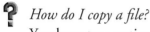 *How do I move a file?*
You have two options:
A) Select a file and use the Move dialog from the **File | Copy** menu
option to specify the destination drive and/or directory.
B) Select a file and then drag it to the new sub-directory or drive.

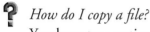 *How do I delete a file?*
Select a file and then press the Delete key or choose the **File | Delete**
option.

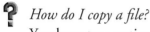 *How do I rename a file?*
Select the file and then choose the **File | Rename** option.

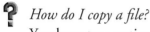 *How do I select multiple files?*
Click on the initial file in the group. Then Shift-click on another file. All
files between these two files will be selected. Or, you can Ctrl-click files
to add or delete them individually from the group.

? *How do I create a directory?*
Click on the directory that will contain the new directory, then choose
the **File | Create Directory** option. Enter the name of the new directory
in the dialog that appears.

? *How do I associate a file with an application?*
*How do I make it so that when I double-click on a file it automatically pops
up in the right application?*
Say you want to be able to double-click on TXT files in the File Manager
and have them automatically load in the Notepad application. Click on
any TXT file. Choose the **File | Associate** option. In the list that appears,
select the Notepad application.

? *I know that what is shown in the window is not right (e.g., you know you
just copied a file and it's not there, or its size shows as zero, or the display
doesn't refresh after you swap floppy disks). How do I refresh the display?*
Click on the drive icon once and the File Manager will reread the directory for that disk and refresh the display. If nothing happens, then close
all windows and make sure you don't have two or more windows open
for the same drive. If you do, close all but one and then click on the drive
icon.

? *How do I format a floppy disk?*
Put the disk in a drive. Choose the **Disk | Format Disk** option. Choose
the proper drive and the correct capacity. If you want to label the disk,
enter the label. Quick formatting quickly clears out the FAT on a previously formatted disk.

? *I can see how to format a floppy disk, but how do I format a hard disk?*
Use the Format command in the MS-DOS window.

? *How do I get rid of the confirmation dialog every time I copy a file?*
Choose the **Confirmation** option in the Options menu. Click the **Help**
button for a quick description of the possibilities.

? *Is it possible to make the font bigger? The file names are hard to read on my
screen.*
Use the **Options | Font** option.

How do I connect to other drives on the network?
See Chapter 5.

How do I secure my files so that other people can't read them?
See Chapter 5.

How do I view hidden files?
Use the **View | By File Type** option.

4.7 Tips

To select groups of files across separate directories, use the **Search** option in the File menu. It will collect files into the search window, and you can select those files for movement or copying to another directory or drive. For example, you can delete all the BAK files on a drive by searching for them, selecting all the resulting files in the search window, and then deleting them with the Delete key or the **File | Delete** option.

Use Ctrl-drag to copy files from directory to directory in the same way you normally move files. Click on the file(s) first to select them, then Ctrl-drag them.

To copy files in the same directory–for example, to duplicate a file to back it up–use the **File | Copy** option and enter the new file name in the second text area.

You can rename a group of files easily in NT. For example, if you use **File | Select** to select the files named `report.*`, you can rename the entire group to `stats.*` with the **File | Rename** option.

To view hidden files, use the **View | By File Type** option and select the **Hidden Files** check box. Once the file is visible in the File Manager, you can make it permanently visible by selecting the **Files | Properties** option and un-marking the **Hidden** attribute.

4.8 Details

4.8.1   The File menu

The File menu lets you perform operations on individual or groups of files.

4.8.1.1   The File | Open Option

If the selected file is associated with an application, this option will execute the application with that file (see section 4.8.1.9 for more information).

4.8.1.2   The File | Move Option

This option lets you move the selected file(s) or directory(s) to a new directory or drive. An alternative is to drag the files.

4.8.1.3   The File | Copy Option

The Copy option lets you copy selected files or directories to another directory or drive, or within the same directory. You can also copy a file to the Clipboard if it has an association. An alternative is to Ctrl-drag the files on the same drive. Dragging across drives automatically copies the files.

4.8.1.4   The File | Delete Option

This option deletes the selected files. The Delete key does the same thing.

4.8.1.5   The File | Rename Option

This option lets you rename the selected file.

4.8.1.6   The File | Properties Option

The Properties option lets you set and clear attribute bits for the selected files. The attribute bits in the FAT file system are: Hidden, System, Read only, and Archive. This option also displays the location and size of the file (see Figure 4.6).

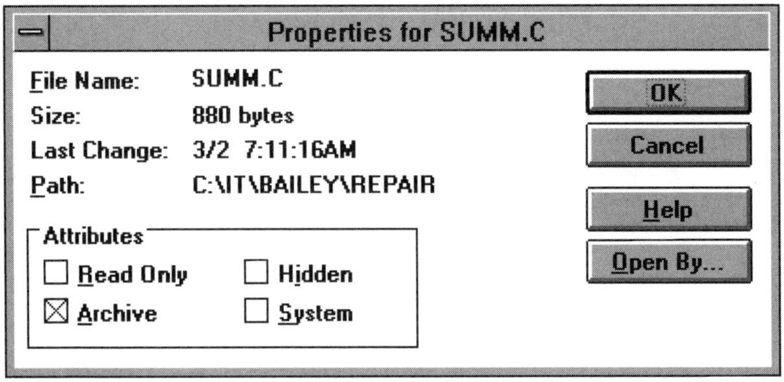

Figure 4.6
The Properties dialog.

4.8.1.7   The File | Run Option

This option lets you execute a command line command from within the File Manager (see Chapter 7 for details on available commands in NT).

4.8.1.8   The File | Print Option

This option will print the file if its type is associated with an application (see section 4.8.1.9 for information on associations).

4.8.1.9   The File | Associate Option

This option lets you associate an application with a file extension. For example, you can associate the Notepad application with files having a TXT extension or a bitmap file with a Paint program. Once an association has been formed, you can double-click on a file with the appropriate extension to execute it under its application. You can also print or open the file using the corresponding options in the File menu (see Figure 4.7).

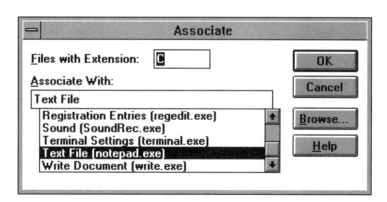

Figure 4.7
The Associate dialog.

4.8.1.10   The File | Create Directory Option

This option lets you create a directory. The new directory is created as a sub-directory of the current directory.

4.8.1.11   The File | Search Option

The Search option lets you examine part or all of the directory tree of a specific drive for files matching the search string. You can search for exact matches, or use the "*" and "?" wild card characters. For example, "*.txt" finds all TXT files, while "??.bmp" finds all bitmap files having two-character-long file names.

4.8.1.12   The File | Select Files Option

This option lets you select groups of files in the current directory. You can use the "*" or "?" wild card characters to specify the group. For example, "*.*" selects all files in the directory; "*.h" Selects all files having an "h" extension. The "?" character matches individual characters. For example, if you've produced reports yearly with names like "report81.txt", then the string "report??.txt" will select those files.

4.8.1.13   The File | Exit Option

This option terminates the File Manager application.

4.8.2   The Disk Menu

The Disk menu lets you format disks, attach to network drives, and so on. Many of these options are discussed in the networking section of Chapter 5.

4.8.2.1   The Disk | Copy Disk Option

The Copy Disk option lets you copy from one disk to another. You will be prompted to insert the source and destination disks as necessary to complete the copy.

4.8.2.2   The Disk | Label Disk Option

This option lets you change the volume label on the current drive. The volume label is a text string that identifies the volume.

4.8.2.3   The Disk | Format Floppy Option

This option formats a floppy disk. You can choose the drive and format in the dialog and you can also specify that a previously formatted disk be quick formatted. Quick formatting replaces only the file allocation table on the disk and is therefore much quicker than a complete format. (See Figure 4.8.)

4.8.2.4   The Disk | Connect Network Drive Option

See Chapter 5.

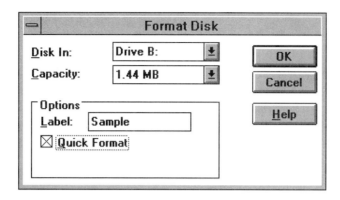

Figure 4.8
The Format dialog.

4.8.2.5 The Disk | Disconnect Network Drive Option

See Chapter 5.

4.8.2.6 The Disk | Share As Option

See Chapter 5.

4.8.2.7 The Disk | Stop Sharing Option

See Chapter 5.

4.8.2.8 The Disk | Select Drive Option

This option presents a dialog that lets you select a drive from a list. This is useful when the mouse is disabled or missing. Normally it's easier to double-click on the drive icon.

4.8.3 The Tree Menu

The Tree menu lets you control the behavior of the directory tree displayed on the left side of any window in the File Manager.

4.8.3.1 The Tree | Expand One Level Option

This option "expands a branch." If the current directory contains sub-directories, they are displayed in the tree. This option applies only to the first level of sub-directories in the current directory. Double-clicking on a directory in the tree does the same thing (see Figures 4.9a and 4.9b and Section 4.8.3.5).

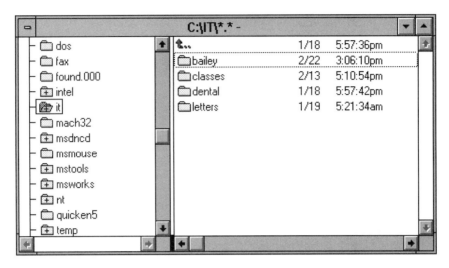

Figure 4.9a
Before expanding an expandable branch.

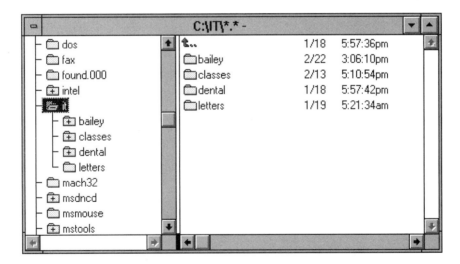

Figure 4.9b
After expanding the branch.

4.8.3.2   The Tree | Expand Branch Option

This option does almost the same thing as **Tree | Expand One Level**, but it displays *all* sub-directories in the current directory rather than just the first level.

4.8.3.3   The Tree | Expand All Option

This option expands all the sub-directories in all directories so they are visible in the tree.

4.8.3.4   The Tree | Collapse Branch Option

This option closes a set of sub-directories. An alternative is to double-click on an open branch in the directory tree.

4.8.3.5   The Tree | Indicate Expandable Branches Option

If this option is selected then any directory that contains sub-directories will be displayed with a plus sign inside the folder icon.

4.8.4   The View Menu

This menu lets you modify your view of the files you see in a drive's window.

4.8.4.1   The View | Tree and Directory Option

If this option is selected, then the drive's window displays the directory tree in the left side of the window and the files for the selected sub-directory in the right side of the window, as shown in Figure 4.10. A black bar at the bottom of each window allows you to change the amount of space given to each side of the window.

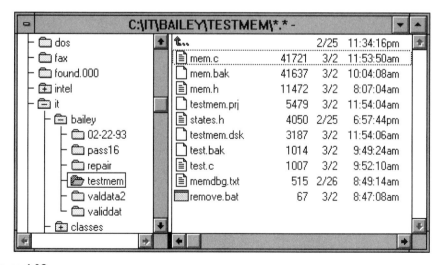

Figure 4.10
The Tree and Directory display.

4.8.4.2   The View | Tree Only Option

This option causes only the directory tree to be displayed in the drive's window (the left side of Figure 4.10).

4.8.4.3   The View | Directory Only Option

This option causes only the contents of the current directory to be displayed in the drive's window (the right side of Figure 4.10).

4.8.4.4   The View | Split Option

This option allows you to adjust the amount of space devoted to the tree and the directory window. As an alternative, you can also drag the bar at the bottom of the window.

4.8.4.5   The View | Name Option

When this option is selected, only the names of the files in the current directory are displayed. This allows many files to be displayed simultaneously.

4.8.4.6   The View | All File Details Option

When this option is selected, details about each file such as the file size and the creation date are displayed alongside each file name.

4.8.4.7   The View | Partial Details

When you select this option, a dialog box will allow you to customize the file details displayed next to each file name (see Figure 4.11).

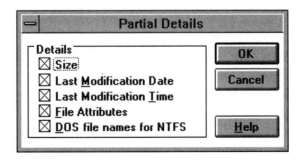

Figure 4.11
The Partial Details dialog.

4.8.4.8   The View | Sort By Name Option

When this option is selected, file names for the default directory are sorted alphabetically by name.

4.8.4.9   The View | Sort by Type Option

When this option is selected, file names for the default directory are sorted alphabetically by extension.

4.8.4.10   The View | Sort by Size Option

When this option is selected, file names for the default directory are sorted by size, large files toward the top.

4.8.4.11   The View | Sort By Date Option

When this option is selected, file names for the default directory are sorted by date.

4.8.4.12   The View | By File Type Option

This option creates a dialog that allows you to choose the types of files displayed in the directory window (see Figure 4.12).

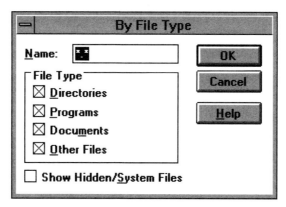

Figure 4.12
The File Type dialog.

4.8.5   The Options Menu

This menu lets you customize the File Manager to suit your individual tastes and needs.

4.8.5.1   The Options | Confirmation Option

The Confirmation option lets you determine which actions in the File Manager are buffered by a confirmation dialog. You can turn off all confirmation dialogs or leave only those you want in place (see Figure 4.13). Click the **Help** button for details about the different options.

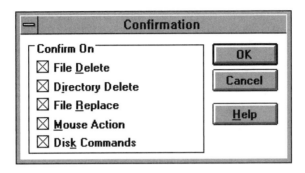

Figure 4.13
The Confirmation dialog.

4.8.5.2   The Options | Font Option

This option lets you choose a different font for displaying file and directory names.

4.8.5.3   The Options | Toolbar Option

This option determines whether or not the Toolbar is displayed.

4.8.5.4   The Options | Drivebar Option

This option determines whether or not the drive icons are displayed.

4.8.5.5   The Options | Status Bar Option

This option determines whether or not the Status bar at the bottom of the window is displayed.

4.8.5.6   The Options | Open New Window on Connect Option

If this option is selected, drive windows are opened for drives when a network connection is made (see Chapter 5).

4.8.5.7   The Options | Minimize on Use Option

When the **Minimize on Use** option is selected, the File Manager will minimize itself after an associated file is launched either with the **File | Open** option or by double-clicking on the file.

4.8.5.8   The Options | Save Settings on Exit Option

When this option is selected, the File Manager will save its state each time it exits or you log off. It will remember which drives you had open and which files were displayed in the drive window.

4.8.6   The Window Menu

This menu lets you easily arrange the windows and icons in the application.

4.8.6.1   The Window | New Window Option

When this option is selected, a new window for the current drive is created. You can scroll the two windows independently and therefore look at the drive in two different ways. An alternative way to do this is to double-click on the drive icon.

4.8.6.2   The Window | Cascade Option

This option will neatly cascade the open windows one on top of the other.

4.8.6.3   The Window | Tile Horizontally Option

This option will neatly tile all open windows horizontally across the File Manager's work area.

4.8.6.4   The Window | Tile Vertically Option

This option will neatly tile all open windows vertically down the File Manager's work area.

4.8.6.5   The Window | Arrange Icons Option

This option will neatly arrange any window icons across the bottom of the File Manager's work area.

4.8.6.6   The Window | Refresh Option

The Refresh option reads the current directories of all open drives and refreshes the tree and directory displays. This step should be taken whenever you think that the File Manager's view of the directory and the directory itself are out of sync. For example, manipulations by other users on a network drive may distort your view of the drive. A synonym for this option is a single click on each drive icon.

4.8.6.7   The Window | 1,2,3... Options

This option lets you recall minimized windows or bring an open window to the top. An alternative is to double-click on the icon or click anywhere in a partially visible window.

4.8.7   The Security Menu

This menu is covered in detail in Chapter 5.

THE FILE MANAGER—
NETWORKS AND SECURITY

5

If your NT machine is attached to a network, you can connect to drives on other NT machines and use them just like any local drive. In certain cases, you can also attach to servers and machines running other operating systems. If your machine uses the NT file system, you can secure your files and directories so they're available only to those people you specify.

This chapter explains how to access networking and security facilities. The Executive Summary explains the rationale behind these facilities.

5.1 Executive Summary

With the advent of powerful desktop workstations, the computing environment at most large companies is changing. Instead of sharing one central machine and hard disk, people now have their own personal machines and their own personal hard disk. They also have access to central servers handling large databases and shared storage resources. Windows NT is a smooth fit in this environment, making it considerably easier for people to get work done.

NT provides two facilities to make network computing easier: 1) network-wide drive sharing, and 2) file security. The drive-sharing portion of NT lets people work in teams, exchanging information back and forth without difficulty. The file security portion prevents unauthorized users from tampering with an individual's files. Just as each person has a lock on his or her file cabinet to prevent people reading or walking off with important files, NT's security system offers the same protection for a hard disk.

The File Manager contains the facilities that allow you to connect to drives on the network, to share your own drives with other network users, and to secure the files on your local hard disk (provided it has been formatted with the NT file system).

The network portion of the File Manager consists of four menu options in the **Disk** menu:

- Connect Network Drive
- Disconnect Network Drive
- Share As
- Stop Sharing

The first option lets you select a drive shared by other network users and attach it to your machine. The second option disconnects a drive to which you are currently connected. The third lets you share your local hard disk, while the fourth lets you stop sharing it. Disk sharing is generally an administrative task so, as a user, you may or may not have the required privileges to share drives (see Appendix C). The use of these options, described in the Guided Tour, is fairly intuitive. Security features allow you to set permissions on files and directories. The **Permissions** option in the **Security** menu of the File Manager lets you use the security system by creating levels of permission on different files and directories. In a secure file system, each file or directory has associated with it:

1. An owner, generally the person who created it (although the Administrator can take ownership at any time).
2. A list of people and groups who can access the file or directory.
3. A list of permissions for each person or group with access to the file. Permissions include the ability to read a file, to write to it, to execute it, and so on.

Every person logging into an NT machine is a member of at least one group. Appendix C contains a discussion that explains the group concept.

If you set permissions on a directory, they can be applied to all sub-directories and files within the directory. You can also specifically select a file and change its particular permissions. The permissions allow groups of users and specific individuals to use your files and directories only in the ways you specify. For example, you can let someone read the file but not write to it. These permissions are available only if your hard disk is formatted for the NT file system.

NT seamlessly combines drive sharing and security features. For example, if you share a drive with everyone but set permissions on a certain directory on that drive, people without permission can't get into that directory. You can also protect drives and directories, even if they do not use the NT file system, by allowing only certain people to access them when they are shared. Since those people must have passwords to get onto other NT machines, you're guaranteed only the right people access the files.

5.2 Guided Tour

This tour will be meaningful to you only if your machine is connected to a network or has the NT file system on its hard disk. The tour is divided into two parts so that you can try out each system separately.

To begin the tour, start the File Manager by double-clicking on its icon in the Program Manager.

5.2.1   The Security System

The NT security system is available on any drive formatted with the NT file system. It lets you pick a file or directory and specify the people who can access it. You can also determine exactly what those people will be able to do.

To try out the security system, access your local drive in the File Manager. Create a new directory (see Chapter 4) called `test` and in that directory create three files by copying random files from elsewhere. Rename the files `file1`, `file2`, and `file3`.

Click on the `test` directory to select it. Now choose the **Owner** option from the **Security** menu. A dialog similar to the one shown in Figure 5.1 appears, telling you you're the owner of the directory (the person who creates a directory or file owns it). You can also use this dialog to check the ownership of any file on the system. If you have the privileges to do so, you can take ownership of files or directories with the **Take Ownership** button.

Figure 5.1
The Directory Permissions dialog.

As the owner of a file or directory, you have the right to set permissions on it. To set permissions, choose the **Permissions** directory in the **Security** menu. You'll see a dialog similar to that shown in Figure 5.2. This dialog shows the permissions currently set for the directory. For example, the dialog in Figure 5.2 shows that the `test` directory has permissions set for the Creator of the file, for Everyone, and for brain. Since Everyone has access, and since that access is Full Access, anyone anywhere on the net can access this directory.

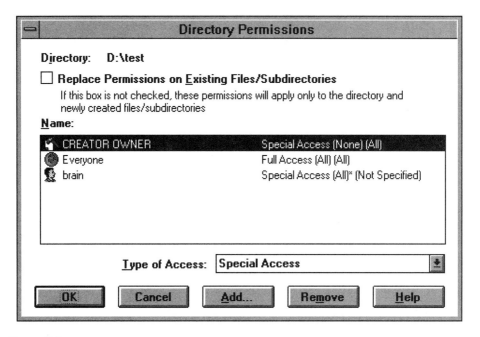

Figure 5.2
The Directory Permissions dialog.

To make the access to this directory more selective, click on Everyone and click the **Remove** button. Now only the Owner and the user called brain can access the file. To add another person or group into the access list, click on the **Add** button. A dialog appears, like the one in Figure 5.3, listing a variety of groups to whom you can give access. For example, you can give access to everyone, to interactive users (all users on this particular machine), users who are members of the Power Users group, and so on. Clicking on the **Show Users** button will include a list of individual users on this machine as well (the **List Names In** combo box at the top of the dialog lets you include user lists from different machines on the net). To give a particular group or user permission to access the `test` directory, for example, click on one of the groups or users.

Now, choose the type of access you want to give them from the **Type of Access** combo box at the bottom of the dialog. You have the following choices: No Access, List, Read, Add, Add and Read, Change, and Full Access. Pick one at random and press OK to return to the Directory Permissions dialog.

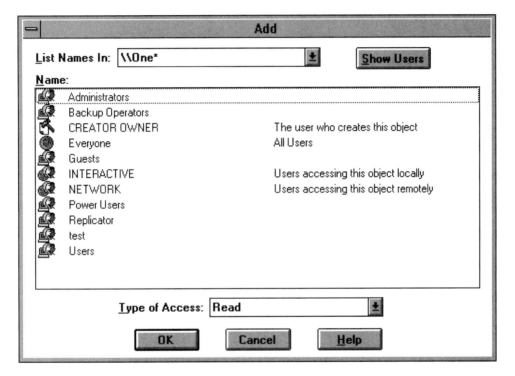

Figure 5.3
The Add dialog.

What were all those different types of access? The six access bits that can be set on any file or directory are self-explanatory:

Read (R)	user can read the file
Write (W)	user can write to the file
Execute (X)	user can execute the file
Delete (D)	user can delete the file
Change Permissions (P)	user can change the access privileges on the file
Take Ownership (O)	user can take ownership of the file

These bits are normally set in combinations. The different access types such as **List**, **Read**, and **Add** in the Add and Directory Permissions dialogs are simply collections of common access bit patterns for the directory (first set of parentheses) and the files in the directory (second set of parentheses). For example, the **List** access type lets the user read and "execute" the directory (which allows you to CD, change directories, into it), but does nothing to the files inside the directory. The user can therefore get a directory listing and see what's there, but can't do anything with the files. **Read** access lets the user see the directory and then read or execute the files.

It's also possible to create your own "special access" types where you set whatever bits you like. You create the list for the directory and the files it contains using the **Special Directory Access** and **Special New File Access** in the Directory Permissions Dialog (see Figure 5.4). For example, if you create a directory that contains executables, and you want to allow people to execute those files but not copy them, you can give the directory permissions R and X and the files permission X.

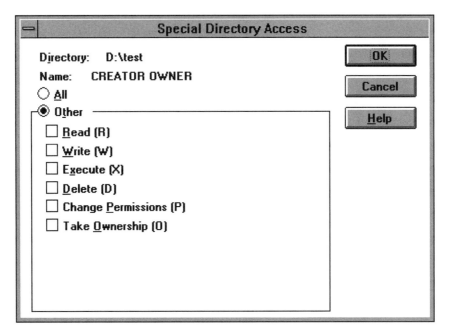

Figure 5.4

The Special Access dialog for directories.

There is a special **No Access** type that is a negative permission. If you give an individual **No Access** permissions then that person will be unable to access the specified file or directory, even if they belong to a group with access.

The Directory Permissions dialog has a check box at the top that lets you percolate permissions set on a directory down through the directory tree, to all files and sub-directories. If you do not set that check box, then any new files or directories created in that directory will inherit the permissions you set, but all existing files will retain their current permissions.

You can set permissions on individual files in the same way you set permissions on a directory. Select the file(s) and then choose the **Permissions** option in the Security menu.

5.2.2   Network Access

One of the most powerful facilities in Windows NT is the ability to connect to other drives on the network through the File Manager. If your machine is on a network you can try out this facility very easily.

Choose the **Connect Network Drive** option in the Disk menu of the File Manager. A dialog appears similar to the one shown in Figure 5.5. Click on the top line in the list box to get a list of domains. Click on the domain name to get a list of machines, and then click on a specific machine to get a list of drives shared by that machine. Next, click on one of the drives. In the Drive combo box you can choose a drive letter to assign to the new drive in the File Manager. Drive letters do not have to be sequential. If you click on the **Reconnect at Logon** check box, this drive will be automatically reconnected each time you log in (if your machine has trouble reconnecting to a drive the next time you log in, because the connected machine is turned off, for example, you'll see a dialog warning of the problem). Press the OK button.

The new drive will appear as a drive icon just like any other drive on your local machine. Double-click on the icon to see the files. If you lack permission to access the files you will see an "access denied" message Otherwise, you should be able to see the files and directories on the drive. You can now use this drive just as you would any other drive on your machine.

If you want to disconnect a drive, choose the **Disconnect Network Drive** option in the Disk menu. Click on the drive in the list that appears and it will disconnect. Numerous permanent connections tend to slow down the time it takes you to log in.

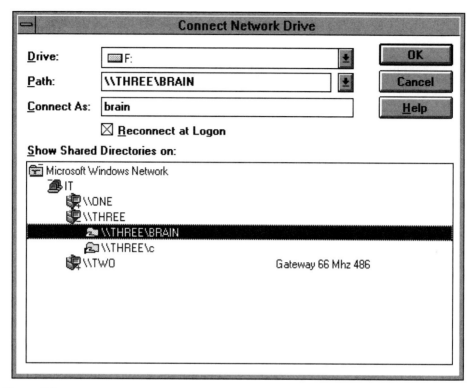

Figure 5.5
The New Connections dialog.

If you are a Power User or Administrator (see Appendix C), then you can share entire drives and specific directories on your machine with others on the network. Select either the root directory of a drive or a specific sub-directory by clicking on it and then select the **Share As** option in the **Disk** menu. A dialog appears similar to the one shown in Figure 5.6. You may specify the name of the drive (a user connecting to the drive will see this name when choosing the connection) and you can also enter a brief description in the Comment field. You can set the maximum number of users who can connect to the drive to limit access.

By pressing the **Permissions** button you can set permissions on the shared drive in the same way that was discussed in Section 5.2.1. If the drive is an NT file system drive, then it probably won't be necessary to set any permissions because all directories will have them already. However, if the drive is a FAT drive, then you may want to set permissions to block access.

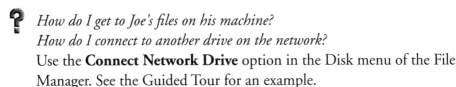

Figure 5.6
The New Share dialog.

If for some reason you have problems sharing a drive, try the **Stop Sharing** option, then eliminate all shares on the drive and try again.

To stop sharing a drive, select the **Stop Sharing** dialog in the Disk menu. To review statistics on shared volumes use the **Server** applet in the Control Panel.

The reason sharing is limited to Administrators is that shared drives are available over the net as soon as the machine is turned on. If all users were allowed to specify shared drives and directories, not only would there be a great deal of duplication but the potentially large number of shares would bog down the machine. Sharing also has security repercussions.

5.3 Common Questions

How do I get to Joe's files on his machine?
How do I connect to another drive on the network?
Use the **Connect Network Drive** option in the Disk menu of the File Manager. See the Guided Tour for an example.

How do I share the drive on my machine with a co-worker?
Use the **Share As** option in the Disk menu of the File Manager. You generally need to be an Administrator to share a drive (see Appendix C and the Guided Tour).

? *How do I restrict access to certain files on my machine?*
With the NT file system you can set permissions on directories and files
using the **Permissions** option in the File menu (see the Guided Tour for
an example).

? *How do I tell who owns a certain file?*
Use the **Owner** option in the Security menu.

5.4 Details

5.4.1 The Disk Menu

The four network options in the Disk menu allow you to connect to network drives and share drives on your machine.

5.4.1.1 The Disk | Connect Network Drive Option

This option lets you connect to a drive or directory on another machine
(see the Guided Tour in Section 5.2.2 for an example).

5.4.1.2 The Disk | Disconnect Network Drive Option

This option lets you Disconnect from a drive to which you have previously
connected.

5.4.1.3 The Disk | Share As Option

If you are an Administrator, this option lets you share a drive or directory on
your machine with other network users (see the Guided Tour in Section 5.2.2).

5.4.1.4 The Disk | Stop Sharing Option

This option lets you stop sharing a drive you previously made available on
the network.

5.4.2 The Security Menu

This menu contains options that let you secure files and directories on a
drive formatted for the NT file system.

5.4.2.1 The Security | Permissions Option

This option lets you set specific permissions on a file or directory (see sections 5.1 and 5.2 for an example of this, as well as the rationale behind it).

5.4.2.2   The Security | Owner Option

This option displays a dialog that tells you who owns a file or directory. If you have permission to do so, you can take ownership of the file with the **Take Ownership** button in this dialog.

THE PRINT MANAGER

It seems that no matter how well NT workstations are interconnected across the network, and no matter how badly we'd like to create a paperless office, almost every computer-created document ends up printed on paper. This tendency makes printers a very important resource. In NT, the Print Manager is your connection to the different printers available on your machine and over the network.

6.1 Executive Summary

The Print Manager either lets you print on printers connected directly to your machine, or on printers made available by other NT workstations on the network. There are three things you can do in the Print Manager:

1. You can control documents that have been released to the printer if you have the proper permissions. For example, you can delete a document from the printer queue, pause printing to add paper to the printer, or move the position of a printout in the queue. You can also retrieve a detailed set of facts about each document in the queue.

2. You can connect to printers that are shared on the network.

3. If you have adequate privileges, you can connect new printers to your machine, install their drivers, and share them over the network. You can also assign permissions to the printer using the same security concepts you learned in Chapter 5 (e.g., you can allow and disallow certain users and groups to access a given printer). For example, some users may only be able to print, while others can move items around in the printer queue and delete them.

The Print Manager easily handles multiple printers and lets you direct each type of output to the best available device. You can specify a certain type of form for each printer, and for each tray in a multi-tray printer.

6.2 Guided Tour

Start the Print Manager by double-clicking on its icon in the Main group of the Program Manager. You'll see a window similar to the one shown in Figure 6.1. This figure shows a status window for a printer named "old" which is directly connected to the machine, as well as a printer called "epson" which is shared over the network by the machine named "one." In your Print Manager you may or may not see status windows, depending on how your machine and network are configured.

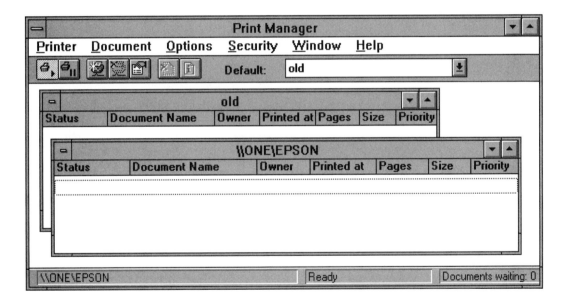

Figure 6.1
The Print Manager.

To experience the Print Manager, you need: A) something to print, and B) a printer to print it on. Start by finding a printer. If there is one attached to your machine and set up properly, then you'll see a window for it in the Print Manager. If not, you can try to connect to a printer over the network. The process is identical to connecting to a disk drive over the net as described in Chapter 5.

Choose the **Connect to Printer** option in the **Printer** menu and you'll see a list of machines in the dialog box that appears. Each machine may or may not have printers associated with it. In some cases the printers will all be visible, while in others you may have to double-click on individual machines to see if anything's attached. As printers are exposed, single-click on them to view information about each one in the area at the bottom of the dialog. Choose a printer by double-clicking on it or by single-clicking and pressing the OK button. A status window for the printer will appear in the Print Manager.

Now create something to print. This is easier said than done since we have not covered any applications yet. So, try this: double-click on the Notepad icon in the Accessories group of the Program Manager. Notepad is a simple text editor. Type something into the editor and then choose the **Print** option in the File menu. If all goes well the printout will appear on the default printer. You can change the default printer by using the **Print Setup** option in the File menu of the Notepad application, or by using the Default combo box in the Toolbar of the Print Manager.

If you would like to try out the document handling features of the Print Manager, queue up several fairly long printouts in rapid succession. Look at the status window for the default printer to see a list of the queued printouts. Select one and use the **Remove Document** option in the Document menu. Select another and choose the **Details** option in the same menu. Try pausing and resuming the top printout using the **Pause** and **Resume** options in the Document menu (the equivalently named options in the Printer menu control the entire printer instead of a document). You can also move documents around in the queue, changing the queue order by dragging them to new positions. If you do not have adequate permission to perform any of these operations on the printer in question, you can talk to your Administrator or log in as Administrator and change the permissions yourself (see Appendix C).

Creating and sharing new printers is an administrative task. When you create a new printer you connect it to a port on the machine, load in appropriate drivers, and adjust the printer's details. Figure 6.2 shows the Details dialog. The most interesting feature in this dialog is its ability to control the exact times of printer availability so people can't use the printer when it's locked up or unattended.

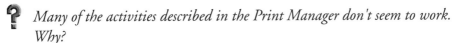

Figure 6.2
The Printer Details dialog.

As Administrator you can also set up specific permissions on a printer. Using the same sorts of dialogs seen in Chapter 5 to manage file permissions, you can select individuals or groups and specify their access to the printer. You can select No Access, Print, Manage Documents, and Full Control access for any user or group. Generally, you want to give the group Everyone normal Print access. If the printer is optimized for a certain task (e.g., a 1,200 DPI laser printer for the marketing department), however, then you may want to limit access to a certain group of users (see Chapter 5 for a discussion of groups).

6.3 Common Questions

 How do I print a document?
Generally you can choose the **Print** option in the File menu of the application and then forget it. The Print Manager will handle everything if it's set up properly.

 Many of the activities described in the Print Manager don't seem to work. Why?
If you lack adequate permission, then many of the menu items in the Print Manager won't work. For example, only people with the proper permission (the Administrator and members of the Print Operators and Power User groups) can create a new printer and share it on the network.

Only individuals or groups given access to the printer can print on it. Many of the options in the Document menu are unavailable unless you have Full Access permission on the printer.

? *How do I remove a printout from the queue?*
Select the printout in the status window for the printer and choose the **Remove Document** option in the Document menu. If the option is not available, see question 2.

? *How do I connect to a printer on another machine?*
Choose the **Connect to Printer** option in the Printer menu. Choose a printer by double-clicking on a machine in the dialog and selecting the appropriate printer.

? *How do I connect a new printer to my machine or change the drivers?*
Use the **Printer | Create Printer** option. You will probably need to be the Administrator on the machine to do this (see Appendix C).

6.4 Details

Many of the options described below are available only if you are the Administrator or have the proper permissions on a given printer.

6.4.1   The Printer Menu

The Printer menu lets you add new printers to your machine, control those printers, and connect to other printers over the network.

6.4.1.1   The Printer | Connect To Printer Option

This option lets you connect to printers shared by other NT machines on the network. It presents a dialog that displays all the machines available on the network. You can double-click on a machine to see its printers and then double-click on the printer to connect. The new printer will be given a status window.

6.4.1.2   The Printer | Create Printer Option

This option lets you connect a new printer to your machine. In the dialog you give the printer a name, select the appropriate driver for it, describe the printer, and specify a port for it. You can also opt to share the printer on the network (if you do so, be sure to check the **Security | Permissions** option).

Clicking the **Details** button lets you specify the times of printer availability and a separator file used between printouts, as well as such things as the priority and printer pools.

6.4.1.3   The Printer | Remove Printer Option

This option removes a printer so it's no longer available on the local machine or the network.

6.4.1.4   The Printer | Properties Option

This option looks just like the **Create Printer** option described above. It's used to modify the properties of a printer after creation.

6.4.1.5   The Printer | Forms Option

Printers, or individual trays on printers, can be dedicated to certain types of forms. For example, you might dedicate a printer to printing labels or printing an inventory form, or you can dedicate a specific tray to envelopes. This option lets you create new form types and view existing forms. You specify a form for a printer in the **Printer | Properties** option by clicking the **Setup** button.

6.4.1.6   The Printer | Pause Option

This option pauses a printer. Choose the printer to pause by selecting its status window. Make sure that no documents are selected in the window by pressing the space bar. Then choose this option.

6.4.1.7   The Printer | Resume Option

This option resumes a paused printer.

6.4.1.8   The Printer | Purge Printer Option

This option deletes all documents in the print queue for the specified printer.

6.4.1.9   Printer | Server Viewer Option

If you have the appropriate privileges, you can use this option to administer printers on other machines on the network. Once you select a machine, your menu selections affect that machine.

6.4.1.10   The Printer | Exit Option

This option terminates the Print Manager.

6.4.2   The Document Menu

This menu lets you control documents in the print queue.

6.4.2.1   The Document | Remove Document Option

This option deletes a document from the queue. Select a document in the status window and then choose this option.

6.4.2.2   The Document | Details Option

This option prints details about the selected document (see Figure 6.3).

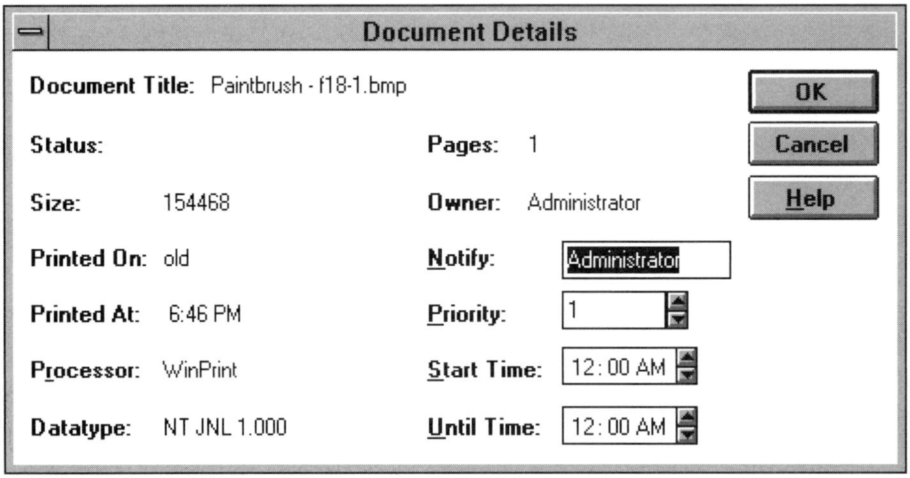

Figure 6.3
The Details dialog.

6.4.2.3   The Document | Pause Option

This option pauses the selected document.

6.4.2.4   The Document | Resume Option

This option resumes the paused printout.

6.4.2.5   The Document | Restart Option

This option reprints the selected document starting at the beginning. It is extremely handy after a printer jam forces you to throw out the document and start over.

6.4.3   The Options Menu

This menu lets you control the appearance of the Print Manager.

6.4.3.1   The Options | Toolbar Option

This option toggles the Toolbar on and off.

6.4.3.2   The Options | Status Bar Option

This option toggles the Status bar on and off.

6.4.3.3   The Options | Save Settings On Exit Option

This option causes settings to be saved to disk each time the Print Manager exits.

6.4.4   The Security Menu

This menu lets you secure a printer and monitor its use.

6.4.4.1   The Security | Permissions Option

This option lets you give individuals and groups access to a printer connected to your machine. The dialog shows you who currently has access and what they're allowed to do. You can add new individuals and groups by pressing the **Add** button. The **List Names From** combo box in the **Add** dialog lets you view lists of users or groups on other machines. The **Show Users** dialog shows individual users. Select a group or individual and then select the type of access in the **Type of Access** dialog as follows:

- No Access: the selected group or user will not be allowed to use the printer.
- Print: The user or group can print documents but nothing else.
- Manage Document: The user or group can use the options in the Document menu.
- Full Control: The user or group can set permissions, take ownership of the printer, and so on.

6.4.4.2   The Security | Auditing Option

This option lets you retrieve information about the past use of the printer.

6.4.4.3   The Security | Owner Option

This option shows you the current owner of the printer and lets you take control of the printer if you have permission.

6.4.5   The Window Menu

This menu lets you easily arrange the windows and icons in the application.

6.4.5.1   The Window | Cascade Option

This option will neatly cascade the open windows one on top of the other.

6.4.5.2   The Window | Tile Horizontally Option

This option will neatly tile all open windows horizontally across the Print Manager's work area.

6.4.5.3   The Window | Tile Vertically Option

This option will neatly tile all open windows vertically down the Print Manager's work area.

6.4.5.4   The Window | Arrange Icons Option

This option will neatly arrange any window icons across the bottom of the Print Manager's work area.

6.4.5.5   The Window | Refresh Option

This option forces a refresh on the status windows of all printers.

6.4.5.6   The Window | 1, 2, 3, ... Options

This option lets you recall minimized windows or bring an open window to the top. An alternative is to double-click on the icon or click anywhere in a partially visible window.

THE MS-DOS PROMPT

7

In theory, you should not need a command line interface for Windows NT. The Apple Macintosh, for example, has survived almost 10 years without one. Certain tasks, however, are much easier to accomplish from a command line than they are with a mouse. Also, Windows NT can run the thousands of character-based MS-DOS programs that pre-date Microsoft Windows, as well as character-based programs from OS/2 and POSIX environments. All these tasks are handled in the command line interface embodied in the MS-DOS prompt.

In this chapter we discuss the basic commands available in the MS-DOS box running under Windows NT. If you already know DOS, you'll find these commands very similar to those in standard MS-DOS.

7.1 Executive Summary

The MS-DOS prompt in Windows NT emulates an MS-DOS command interpreter. Figure 7.1 shows a typical DOS window.

If you are moving to NT from an operating system like UNIX, where the command set is incredibly rich and the scripting language is as powerful as most programming languages, you'll find the DOS command set and the batch programming language somewhat lacking. You will probably want to acquire a third party C-shell and UNIX command emulator. On the other hand, if you already know DOS, or if you are coming from an environment with minimal command line capabilities like the Macintosh, the NT command interpreter should seem just fine.

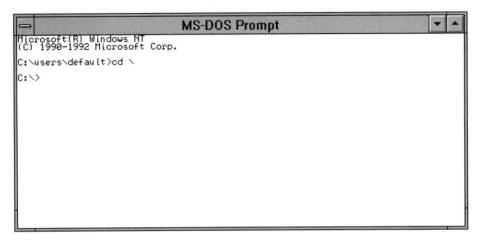

Figure 7.1
The MS-DOS Window.

In general, the command line interface simply gives you another way to do things. For example, there are commands to copy files (COPY), list directories (DIR), rename files (RENAME), delete files (DELETE or ERASE), change file attributes, and so on. These are the same things you would normally do in the File Manager. However, there are commands available in the command line interface that can only be accomplished there. For example, you can search for a string inside a collection of files from the command line (FIND and FINDSTR), or compare two files for differences (FC and COMP). Neither of these capabilities is available anywhere else.

The command line interface also includes a scripting capability known in PC parlance as *batch files*. Batch files let you create collections of commands in a single file. The commands can contain **if** statements and crude loops. These script files must have file names that end with a BAT extension, and they are executed just like any other command. This capability gives you a way to simplify repetitive tasks and is summarized in section 7.5.

7.2 Guided Tour

Start up a DOS window by double-clicking on the MS-DOS icon in the Main group in the Program Manager. Click on the System menu (the small square at the left end of the Title Bar), or press Alt-space. Figure 7.2 shows a typical System menu for a DOS window.

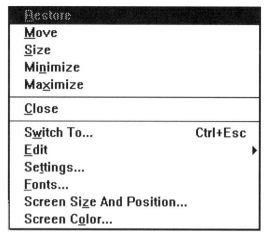

Figure 7.2
The DOS window's System menu.

The System menu contains all the normal options, plus several more that let you customize the window:

The **Fonts** option lets you choose a different font from the available list. If you click on the **Save** check box, the font will be saved automatically and used the next time you invoke a DOS window.

The **Screen Size and Position** option lets you select the number of lines remembered by the DOS window. For example, if you request a 200 line DOS window, a scroll bar appears on the right side of the window and you can scroll backwards up to 200 lines to review your session. The size and position settings can be saved by clicking on the appropriate check box.

The **Screen Color** option lets you choose your favorite screen colors for the DOS window and save that configuration.

The **Settings** option lets you change the window between a full screen and a windowed display (Alt-enter does the same thing), and also allows you to terminate a recalcitrant window. This capability is important when a command hangs and refuses to accept the Ctrl-break or Ctrl-C keystrokes. The normal way to terminate a DOS window is to type "exit" at the command prompt.

The **Edit** option lets you mark sections of the command window so you can copy and paste them elsewhere. To start a copy operation, select the **Copy** option. Move the cursor to the upper left corner of the rectangle you wish to copy using the arrow keys. Then, with the Shift key held down, move the cursor to the rectangle's bottom right corner and it will be highlighted. When you release the Shift key, the selected text is copied to the Clipboard and you can then paste it anywhere you like. It's also possible to paste from the Clipboard into the command window.

There are a variety of commands available in the DOS window. Each is explained in the Details section below, but you can quickly learn a lot about them simply by trying them out.

Look at the DOS window. It's displaying a prompt of some kind, most likely the current drive and directory (you can change the prompt with the PROMPT command). Type "dir" at the command prompt. This is a harmless command that lists the current directory on screen. Type "help dir" to get a listing of its different options and try some out. For example, you can type "dir /os" to get a directory listing sorted by size.

Type "help" to get a list of the available commands along with a one-line description of each. The HELP command displays the list one screen at a time. Press any key to move to the next screen, and press Ctrl-break or Ctrl-C to kill the listing midstream.

To change the current working directory use the CD command. For example, to move up one level in the directory tree type "cd .." (if you're unfamiliar with directory trees see the side-bar in Chapter 4). To move into a directory, type "cd dirname" (replacing "dirname" with the actual directory name). You can easily view the directory names in a file listing produced by the DIR command. In a standard listing each directory name is followed by the string "<DIR>" and, if you use the "/w" option (forward slash w), the directories are enclosed in brackets.

You can change the current drive by typing the drive letter followed by a colon. For example, typing "a:" changes the default drive to drive A. If this is a floppy disk drive, and no disk is in the drive, you'll get an error message stating as much. If there is a disk in the drive, typing "dir" produces a directory listing for the A drive.

Return to drive C by typing "c:". Type "dir" to get a file listing and locate a small file (the file size, in bytes, immediately follows the file name). You can copy that file using the COPY command. For example, if the file you located is called "paper.txt," you can copy it to a file named "junk" by typing "copy paper.txt junk." If you want to copy the file to drive A, type "copy paper.txt a:." To rename it while copying type "copy paper.txt a:junk." In general, you can copy the file from any directory to any other directory by stating the explicit path, as in: "copy d:\bin\apps\paper.txt e:\tmp\remind."

You can delete the file named "junk" by typing "erase junk," if junk is contained in the current directory. If it isn't, you can specify an explicit path (e.g., "erase c:\bin\apps\junk").

Look through the list in Section 7.6 and try out some of the other commands. Learn about the available command options by getting help for each command. For example, if you want to get information about the FC command, type "help fc." You should find that the commands are straightforward and easy to understand. Alternately you can use Windows Help (see Section 7.5.3 for more information).

7.3 Common Questions

Is there a Help file for the commands?
Yes, and it's an extremely good one named `ntcmds.hlp`. The Main group in the Program Manager should contain an icon for it. If not, use the File Manager to search for the file and then double-click on the file directly, create your own icon for it, or type "winhlp32 ntcmds.hlp" at the command line.

How do I change the font for the command window?
Use the **Fonts** option in the System menu for the command window. The System menu is activated by clicking on the small square on the left of the Title Bar or by pressing Alt-space.

Is there a way to have the command window store more than 25 lines so that I can scroll backwards?
Use the **Settings** option in the System menu. The System menu is activated by clicking on the small square on the left of the Title Bar or by pressing Alt-space.

I have a file name containing blanks in the NT file system. How do I reference it on the command line?
Let's say you have a file in the NT file system named "my file," and you want to copy it to a file named "temp." You can't type "copy my file

junk" because the space in the file name is misinterpreted. To solve this problem, wrap the file name in quotes as shown below:

```
copy "my file" junk
```

An alternate solution is to avoid file names containing blanks.

How do I cut and paste from the DOS window?
Use the **Edit** option in the System menu and follow the instructions listed in the Guided Tour.

What commands are available in the DOS window?
Type "help" for a list of the available commands, or look at the listing in Section 7.5.8.

I have an old DOS program that I want to run under NT. How do I do that?
Load the program onto the system and type its name at the command line. The program should run just fine. If you like, you can create a PIF file for it and use it to tune NT's handling of the program (see Chapter 2).

When I type a certain command the system prints a "command not found" message instead of executing it. But it's there because when I type an explicit path to it, it executes. How can I make it so I don't have to type the explicit path to the command each time?
There is an *environment variable* called PATH that controls where NT searches for commands. If you place a directory in the PATH variable, NT automatically searches that directory, along with all the other directories specified, whenever you request a command (see Section 7.5.7 for more information).

7.4 Tips

If you need to execute the same set of commands over and over again, use a batch file (see Section 7.5 for details).

If you use a DOS window every time you log in, add the icon to your Start-up group in the Program Manager so the window is always available.

If you need to run a command or a batch file often, and you want to create an icon for it in the Program Manager, you can do so. See Section 2.6.1.1

for a description of how to create a new Program Item. Set the Command
Line field to the command and any parameters that need to be applied. An
alternative is to create a PIF file for the command and run it using an icon
that points to the PIF file (see the PIF side-bar in Chapter 2).

The NT file system allows file names to contain blank characters. To access
these file names on the command line, wrap the file name in double
quotes.

7.5 Commands and Batch Files

This section provides details about the DOS interpreter built into Windows NT. Details on the options for each command are available in the on-line
Help. This section, combined with the details contained in the Help files, will
give you all the information you need (see Section 7.5.3 for details on finding
and using the on-line Help).

If you are coming from DOS, Section 7.5.1 outlines some basic differences
between the NT command window and a standard DOS prompt. If you are
coming from a UNIX environment, Section 7.5.2 contains a table of command
equivalents.

7.5.1   Differences Between NT and DOS

If you are moving to NT from a DOS or Windows 3.1 platform, you'll
notice some differences in the Windows NT DOS prompt. For instance, there
is no longer a `command.com` file. In NT the command interpreter is called
`cmd.exe`. Overall, DOS users should be completely comfortable with the
DOS window in NT, but there are some changes you should know about.

The DOS prompt in NT is completely simulated. NT does not "sit on
top of" DOS like Windows does. NT is its own operating system, and it sim-
ulates DOS. This simulation allows you to run DOS programs on any NT
platform. For example, if NT is running on a MIPS RISC processor, you can
still run DOS programs and DOS commands there because the Intel architec-
ture is simulated on any non-Intel platform.

One of the nicest additions to the NT version of DOS is the START
command. This command can be placed in front of any other command to run
it in the background. For example, if you type "start notepad," the Windows

NT Notepad application will begin execution as a separate task, and the command line will return ready to accept another command.

Windows NT has augmented many of the standard DOS commands and also added some new commands of its own. For example, familiar commands like MORE and DEL now have more command switches. In most cases the new switches make the commands more "UNIX-like." The MORE command, for instance, has a new "/e" option that makes it act a lot like the UNIX MORE command. The list below names the commands that have changed or been added:

at, cmd, convert, del, dir, diskcopy, diskcomp, echoconfig, emm, endlocal, findstr, format, keyb, label, mode, more, move, path, popd, print, pushd, recover, setlocal, sort, start, title, xcopy, winver, &&, | |, &, ( ), ^

Many commands found in standard DOS have been removed. For example, ASSIGN is no longer available, since you can do the same thing in the File Manager. Things like MIRROR and FASTOPEN have been removed because NT already does the same thing automatically. The following commands are not available in NT:

assign, ctty, dosshell, expand, fastopen, fdisk, join, mirror, sys, undelete, unformat

NT also provides a few extra capabilities in batch files such as && and ||. These are UNIX-isms copied over to make UNIX transplants feel more comfortable.

Finally, the `autoexec.bat` and `config.sys` files are not nearly so important in Windows NT. They can be used, but many of the `config.sys` drivers and commands used in standard DOS are simply ignored by NT. If your configuration depends on these files in DOS, then you'll want to do some research and make sure NT handles the capabilities they provided in a similar manner. Look in the NT documentation for a discussion of the autoexec and config files.

The Help file (see Section 7.5.3) contains a list of major changes in the NT DOS prompt. You will want to review these changes briefly just so you're aware of them.

7.5.2   UNIX Equivalents

The following table gives the equivalent DOS command for many common UNIX commands. In some cases the equivalent command is only a vague approximation of the UNIX command, but it points you in the right direction. Use the Windows NT Help file in the Main group of the Program Manager to find out more about the DOS commands:

UNIX	DOS
at, cron	at
alias	doskey
cat	type
cd	cd
chmod	attrib
clear	cls
cp	copy
cp -r	xcopy
csh, sh	cmd
date	date, time
diff	comp, fc
echo	echo
exit	exit
foreach	for
ftp	ftp
goto	goto
grep	find, findstr
if	if
lpr	print
ls	dir
.login	Startup group, Login script
man	help
mkdir	mkdir
more	more
path	path
ping	ping
pushd	pushd
popd	popd

rm	del, erase
rmdir, rm -rf	rmdir
rsh	rsh
setenv	set
shift	shift
sort	sort
telnet	telnet
#	rem
&	start

7.5.3   Command Options and Help

NT provides two different types of Help for the command line interface. First, an extensive windows-style Help file is available. You should find an icon for this Help file in the Main group of the Program Manager. If not, search for `ntcmds.hlp` and make your own. The file contains detailed descriptions of each command and its options, as well as a good glossary of NT terms and concepts (click on the **Glossary** button).

Help is also available at the command line itself. If you type "help," you'll see a listing containing a one-line summary of each command available in NT. You can also follow the Help command with a specific command (e.g., "help dir") and receive a more detailed description of the DIR command and its options. Most commands, when given the "/?" option, will print this same description, so "help dir" and "dir /?" are equivalent.

7.5.4   Common Knowledge

Anyone experienced with DOS has a few pieces of information wired into their brains that have become so automatic they no longer even think about them. If you are coming from a different environment, you need to be aware of these facts to put you on even ground.

The NT file system allows file names of any length. However, if you use floppy disks or connect to FAT file systems over the network, you will have to use the FAT file name conventions that every DOS user knows by heart. File names on the PC have always followed the eight-dot-three format. That is, file names can have up to eight characters, followed by a period, followed by a three-character extension. It's legal to leave off the period and the extension if you like. A file name can contain letters or numbers and a few punctuation characters such as underscores, dashes, and dollar signs. Case does not matter in DOS. Upper and lower case characters are identical. For example, the following file names are valid:

backit.bat

123.exe

report.txt

files.zip

a.lg

hello.doc

makefile

3-93_rpt.txt

By convention, the three-character portion following the dot is called an *extension* and is used to indicate the file type. The following list identifies the most common types:

EXE	executable
COM	executable
TXT	text
BAT	DOS batch file
DLL	dynamic link library
HLP	help file
BMP	bitmap file
WAV	digitized sound file
TMP	temporary file
ZIP	Zip file–a common PC file compression and archiving format

When you want to specify a set of files, you can use two wildcard characters: * and ?. For example, if you want to delete all the files having an OBJ extension in the current directory, you can say "del *.obj", or "del /s *.obj" if you wish to delete from all the sub-directories as well. The "*" indicates that you want to match any set of characters preceding the period. You can also say "del code*.obj." This indicates that any "obj" file beginning with the letters "code" should be deleted. Files such as "code1.obj," "codeexec.obj," and "code_cx.-obj" all fall into this category. The name "*.*" means "all files," whereas the name "*" means "all files without an extension."

The "*" wildcard is not nearly as flexible in DOS as it is, for example, in UNIX. You can place one "*" before the period and one after. This character also should not be used preceding characters. In general, a command such as "dir *abc.*" will not work the way you expect it to work.

The "?" character is used as a single character wildcard. It will match any single character in the specified position. For example, if you have three files named "code1.obj," "code2.obj" and "code3.obj," the command "del code?.obj" will delete all of them but leave files such as "code5a.obj" in place.

DOS organizes files in a tree-structured directory system. Unlike UNIX and most mainframes, which give the user the impression of a single large directory tree regardless of the number of drives implementing it, DOS treats drives as separate entities and assigns them *drive letters*. Section 4.2 contains a description of the typical drive scheme on PCs. For example, you specify the current drive on the command line by typing "C:" (C colon). This makes drive C the default drive.

Each separate drive has a root directory represented by "\" (a backslash). The root directory on drive C, therefore, is known as "C:\." The root directory can contain files and other sub-directories. If the root directory contains a sub-directory named "files," you can make that directory the default by typing "cd c:\files." Each drive has a default directory. Changing into a directory with the CD command makes that directory the default directory for that particular drive. A command that does not specify a particular drive or directory automatically applies to the default drive and its default directory. For example, the DIR command will list the default directory on the current default drive. See the side-bar on directory trees in Chapter 4 for more information.

Any command can normally be terminated during execution either by typing "Ctrl-break" or "Ctrl-C." If that does not work, you can kill the entire DOS window using the **Terminate** button in the **Settings** option in the System Menu.

The DOS window recognizes several keystrokes and handles them with special behavior. The ESC key clears the command line. F3 repeats the last command. F7 presents a history of previous commands in a dialog. The up and down arrow keys on the command line scroll through previous commands.

7.5.5   File Re-direction

All DOS commands that produce text output to the screen or accept text input from the keyboard can have their input and output *re-directed* to and from a file or another command. For example, the DIR command dumps its output to the screen. If you want its output re-directed to a file instead, so you can save it, type "dir > filename," where "filename" is any valid filename. Input is re-directed using the "<" symbol. For example, the SORT command sorts the input stream, so "sort < filename" will sort the contents of the file named by "filename" and then dump the sorted output to the screen. If you then want to re-direct SORT's output as well, the format is "sort <file1 >file2."

Output from one command can be directed into the input of another command with the "|" (pipe) character. For example, "dir | sort" sends the output of the DIR command directly into the input of the SORT command. The output of SORT is dumped to the screen, but it can be subsequently piped or re-directed as well.

7.5.6   Batch Files

DOS supports the concept of *batch files,* which are used to create command scripts. A command script collects together a set of commands that can then be executed by typing the name of the batch file. Batch files can contain any DOS command that you would type on the command line. DOS also defines a set of eight special commands, used only in batch files, that allow branching and repetition, comments, and string output. With these extra commands, batch files allow you to use DOS commands as a simple programming language.

You can create batch files for all the command sequences you use every day. For example, if you write and compile programs you probably back up your current code directory onto a floppy at the end of the day. You might type the following commands each time:

```
erase *.obj
erase *.exe
copy *.* b:
```

By collecting these commands into a batch file you can reduce the amount of typing and save yourself from making unnecessary mistakes. Using the Notepad application (see Chapter 8) you can create a text file named code-

`back.bat` that contains the three commands. The BAT extension indicates to DOS that the text file is a batch file. By typing "codeback" on the command line you execute the batch file. DOS executes the three commands it finds in the file in the order specified. You can also double-click on a batch file in the File Manager to execute it, or you can create an icon for it in the Program Manager.

Batch files can accept command line parameters. This capability allows you to make your command scripts more flexible and general. For example, in the backup utility shown above you can let the user indicate the disk drive at run time by accepting the drive specifier on the command line and substituting it into the COPY command, as shown below:

```
erase *.obj
erase *.exe
copy *.* %1
```

The user would now invoke the batch file by typing "codeback a:" or "codeback b:." The "%1" symbol at the end of the COPY command is a place holder for the first parameter on the command line. When the batch file executes, the first parameter automatically replaces the %1 and then the COPY command executes. A batch file can accept up to nine parameters, labeled "%1" though "%9." You might, for instance, want the batch file to save a directory listing of the current files on the floppy disk, as well as the files themselves. You could hard code that information using the name "manifest" for the directory listing file, as shown below:

```
erase *.obj
erase *.exe
erase manifest
dir > manifest
copy *.* %1
```

Or you can accept the name of the manifest file as a second parameter and code the batch file as follows:

```
erase *.obj
erase *.exe
erase %2
dir > %2
copy *.* %1
```

The user can type "codeback a: filelist.txt" to specify "filelist.txt" as the name of the file list. The "%0" place holder is also defined, and it gets replaced by the name of the batch file itself. It's also possible to create your own variables in batch files (see Section 7.5.7).

DOS defines eight commands that can be used specifically in batch files. These commands add flexibility to the command scripts you create. The eight commands are listed below:

CALL	Calls second batch file like a subroutine.
ECHO	Prints a string to the screen.
FOR	Repeats a command on each of a group of file names.
GOTO	Jumps to a labeled line.
IF	Executes the command that follows if the condition evaluates to true.
PAUSE	Prompts the user to press a key to continue.
REM	Specifies that the line contains a remark (a comment).
SHIFT	Shifts parameters.

The following sections describe each of these commands.

7.5.6.1   The Call Command

The CALL command is used to make a subroutine-like call to a second batch file from an executing batch file. For example, you might have two batch files named a.bat and b.bat as shown below:

a.bat:

```
b
erase %2
dir > %2
copy *.* %1
```

b.bat:

```
erase *.obj
erase *.exe
```

If the user executes a.bat, it immediately executes b.bat. However, when b.bat completes execution it never returns to a.bat. If you want b.bat to return to a.bat, so a.bat can complete its commands, use the statement "call b" as shown below:

a.bat:

```
call b
erase %2
dir > %2
copy *.* %1
```

When b.bat completes, it returns to a.bat like a subroutine so that a.bat can continue execution.

7.5.6.2   The Echo Command

Each time a command is executed in a batch file, that command is echoed on the screen so the user can see what's happening. In many cases this output can be distracting, especially for beginners. By placing the line "echo off" at the top of a batch file, however, you turn echoing off for all commands in the file. You can also turn off the echoing for an individual command by preceding it with an "@" character.

The echo command is also used to display text to the screen during the execution of a batch file. For example, you can use it to display error messages or messages that inform the user of progress. This is demonstrated below:

```
@echo off
echo Beginning backup...
erase *.obj
erase *.exe
erase %2
dir > %2
copy *.* %1
echo Backup complete.
```

The statement "echo ."prints a blank line.

7.5.6.3   The For Command

The FOR command is used to repeat a command across a set of files. For example, if you want to repeat the PRINT command across a set of C program files, the following statement in a batch file will handle it:

```
for %%f (*.c) do print %%f
```

The same statement can be used on the command line by replacing %% with %. The double percents are needed in a batch file because the % character is reserved for parameters.

The variable "f" is used as a place holder for a specific file name. The value(s) inside the parentheses are expanded into a list of files, and "f" is replaced with each file name in turn. You can place any number of file names into the parentheses. For example, the following statement prints all C program and header files, along with the makefile:

```
for %%f (*.c *.h makefile) do print %%f
```

7.5.6.4   The Goto Command

The GOTO command allows a batch file to branch to a label somewhere else in the batch file. A label consists of a colon followed by a string on a line by itself. The following code fragment demonstrates the GOTO command:

```
@echo off
echo starting
goto xxx
echo these lines
echo will be skipped
:xxx
echo done
```

When executed, this batch file produces only the words "starting" and "done" on the screen.

The GOTO command is normally used with the IF command to implement branching.

7.5.6.5   The If Command

The IF command evaluates an expression and, if true, executes a single command. That command may be any DOS command, including GOTO. The following forms are supported:

```
if [not] errorlevel num command
if [not] string1==string2 command
if [not] exist filename command
```

The NOT modifier is optional in all three statements.

The first form checks the error level produced by the execution of the previous command. If the value is greater than or equal to "num," then the condition evaluates true and DOS executes the specified command. All DOS commands return an error level of 0 if successful and then rising numbers for errors of rising severity. For example, the FORMAT command produces an error level of 0 if successful, 3 if the user halted the formatting process with Ctrl-C or Ctrl-break, 4 if some sort of fatal error occurs, or 5 if the user responds with "N" to the question "Proceed with format?." This information is available in the on-line Help file (see Section 7.5.3). The error code is placed in a global variable upon completion of the command and it is this error code that the IF statement is evaluating. The following example demonstrates the use of this form:

```
copy %1 %2
if errorlevel 1 echo Something went wrong.
```

The second form the IF command checks for is equality between strings. For example:

```
if %1==a: format %1
```

This form of the IF statement can also be used to branch to different sections of a batch file based on a command line option. The technique is frequently necessary to create simple menu-driven interfaces. It's also used to detect the number of parameters. For example, the following statement makes sure the user entered at least one parameter:

```
if "%1" == "" goto end
```

The final form checks for existence of a file name:

```
if exist sample.txt goto xxx
```

7.5.6.6   The Pause Command

The PAUSE command temporarily halts the execution of a batch file and prompts the user to press a key to continue. It is frequently used after displaying a message to give the user time to read it, or inside of loops to allow the user to do something before the next iteration begins.

7.5.6.7   The Rem Command

The REM command identifies a remark or comment. The remainder of the line that begins with REM is ignored.

7.5.6.8   The Shift Command

The SHIFT command shifts all parameters "to the left" by one, so %0 is replaced by %1, %1 is replaced by %2, and so on to %9. If the user entered more than 9 parameters, this is a way to access them because %9 is replaced by the 10th parameter. The SHIFT command is also useful in situations where the user may enter an unknown number of parameters. You can continuously check %1 in a loop until it equals "" (See 7.5.6.5).

7.5.7   Environment Variables

NT maintains a set of variables called *environment variables* that control the behavior of the system and the DOS window. They can also be used inside batch files. These variables are set either by using the **System** applet in the Control Panel, or the SET command in DOS. When set in the **System** applet the variables are persistent. Each time you log in they're set for the entire system. If you use the SET command, the variable applies only to the current window.

To see the current values of the environment variables, type "set" on the command line. You can create your own variables on the fly. For example, type "set SAMPLE=hello," and then type "set" to display the list again. There will be a new variable named SAMPLE set to the string "hello." To remove this variable you can type "set SAMPLE=". Remember that this variable is local to this DOS window only, and not to any other DOS window.

You can use environment variables in batch files. For example, if you create the following batch file:

```
set SAMPLE=hello
echo %SAMPLE%
```

You will see the word "hello" appear on the screen when the batch file is executed.

If you want to permanently set an environment variable, call up the **System** applet in the Control Panel as shown in Figure 7.3. Type the name of the variable in the Variable field and the value for it in the Value field. *Be sure to press the **Set** button, and then the OK button.* Variables entered here will be in effect in all DOS windows and also systemwide the next time you log in to NT.

The most common environment variable that the user sets is the PATH variable. Let's say you want to add the "\Apps" directory to your path. You don't want to say "set Path=\Apps" because then you lose your existing path. Instead, you type "set Path=\Apps;%Path%". The semicolon is the separator between different directories in the path. This line appends "\Apps" to the existing path, and applies only to the current window.

You can also append directories to the path in the **System** applet of the
Control Panel. To add "\Apps" to the path, enter "Path" into the Variable field
and "\Apps" in the Value field and press the **Set** and OK buttons. The new directory will be appended to the existing path.

Some commands recognize certain environment variables. For example,
if you create an environment variable named MORE and set it to "\e", the
MORE command will automatically use that command line option any time
it's invoked. Look for details such as these in the on-line Help file.

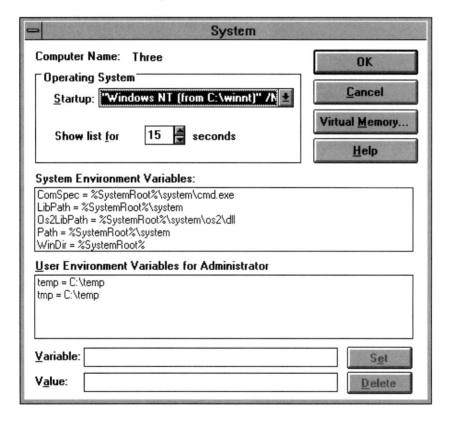

Figure 7.3
The System applet in the Control Panel lets you set environment variables.

7.5.8   Commands

This section summarizes many of the important commands available in
the command window of Windows NT. Its purpose is not to describe each

command in detail; that alone would require a book twice this size. Instead, its purpose is to alert you to the commands that are available so you can look up the details in the on-line documentation. See the HELP command below for details on this documentation.

 AT: Schedules a command for execution at a later time.

Example:
at 8:15 "dir"

 ATTRIB: Lets you view and change file attributes. Similar to the **File | Properties** option in the File Manager.

Examples:
attrib filename   // displays attributes
attrib -h filename   // clears the "hidden" attribute bit

 BREAK: Causes the system to check for Ctrl-break and Ctrl-C sequences (used to halt a command from the command line) more frequently.

Example:
break

 CALL: Allows one batch program to call another. If CALL is not used (e.g., the second batch file is invoked by name in the first batch file instead of using CALL), the batch file will terminate at the end of the second batch file (see Section 7.5.6.1 for an example).

 CD, CHDIR: Lets you change the current working directory. Single-clicking on a directory in the File Manager does the same thing.

Examples:
cd dirname   // sets current directory to current-directory/dirname
cd ..   // sets current directory to parent of current directory
if on the C drive...
cd a:\dirname   // sets the directory on drive A without changing drives
if on the C drive...
cd c:\bin\apps   //sets the current directory to an explicit path

 CHKDSK: Scans the disk for allocation problems and reports on disk usage and problems found. Useful for repairing minor problems caused by aberrant programs or disk errors.

Examples:
chkdsk   // checks current drive

```
chkdsk a:              // checks A drive
chkdsk /f              // repairs damage reported by plain chkdsk
```

CLS: Clears the DOS window.

Example:

cls

CMD: Starts a new command interpreter. Used with START it opens a new DOS window (see below).

Example:

start cmd

COMP: Compares two files. See also FC below.

Example:

comp file1.txt file2.txt

COPY: Copies a file or files from one directory to another. This command cannot copy directories or directory trees (see XCOPY below for that).

Examples:

```
copy file1 file2       // copies file1 to file2
copy file1 a:          // copies file1 to default directory on A
copy file1 a:file2     // copies file1 to drive A and renames it
copy a:file1           // copies file1 on drive A to current directory
copy file1 ..          // copies file1 to parent of current directory
copy c:\bin\apps\file1 a:\tmp // copies file1 (explicitly specified) to a:\tmp
copy *.* a:            // copies all files in current directory to drive A
```

DATE: Lets you set the current date if you have permission. If not, see Appendix C. You can do the same thing using the Time/Date icon in the Control Panel (see Chapter 3 and TIME below).

DEL: Deletes a file or a group of files. This command cannot delete sub-directories; use RMDIR for that. It's much easier to delete files and directories in the File Manager (see also ERASE).

Examples:

```
del file1              // deletes file1
del *.*                // deletes all files in current directory
del a:*.*              // deletes all files in current directory on A
del ..\*.txt           // deletes all text files in parent of current directory
```

DIR: Lets you view a listing of files for the current directory or for a directory you specify. The options available let you sort files in different ways. The File Manager does this automatically.

Examples:
```
dir                  // lists default directory
dir *.txt            // lists only the text files in the current directory
dir a:*.txt          // lists only the text files in the current directory on A
dir ..               // lists all files in parent directory
dir /os              // lists files for default directory sorted by size
```

 DISKCOMP: This command lets you compare identically formatted floppy disks for any differences.

Example:
```
diskcomp a:          // compares two floppy disks and prompts you to swap.
```

 DISKCOPY: Copies the contents of a floppy disk to a second identically formatted floppy disk. This is the same as the **Disk | Copy Disk** option in the File Manager.

Example:
```
diskcopy a:          // copies one floppy to another floppy and prompts you to swap
```

 DOSKEY: This command is invoked automatically in NT. It lets you retrieve commands you've previously entered using the up arrow or F7 keys. It also handles command aliasing.

 ECHO: Used to print messages to the user in batch files (see Section 7.5.6.2 for an example).

 ERASE: Same as DELETE.

 EXIT: Terminates the current command shell. An alternative is to click on the **Terminate** button in the **Settings** option of the System menu.

 FC: Displays the differences between two files. See also COMP.

 FIND, FINDSTR: Lets you search for a string within groups of files. Similar to the GREP capability in UNIX. FINDSTR handles regular expressions, while FIND matches strings literally. See the Help file for a complete description of the regular expression syntax in NT.

Examples:
```
find "hello" *.txt   // prints occurrences of the string hello
```

findstr "h.llo" *.txt   // "." works like "?" in filenames

FOR: Lets you execute a command on each file in a group of files (see Section 7.5.6.3 for an example).

FORMAT: Formats floppy and hard disks. You can specify the file system and, in the case of floppy disks, the density.

Examples:

format a:	// formats the disk in A
format c:	// wipes your hard disk clean and is therefore not an advisable procedure
format d: /f:ntfs	// formats D with NT file system

GOTO: The GOTO command lets you jump to a label in a batch program (see Section 7.5.6.4 for an example).

HELP: If you type "help" by itself, the Help command prints a list of all available commands to the screen, each with a one-line description. If you type "help" followed by a command name, the system will print a description of the specified command followed by a brief description of the command line options. Most commands, when past the "/?" option, will print that same multi-line description.
Much more complete Help is available through the Windows Help system (see Section 1.6). This Help file should have an icon in the Main Group of the Program Manager. If you double-click on this icon, you'll find a very extensive Help file with a complete and thorough glossary of Windows NT terminology, as well as an excellent command index and command descriptions. Use it as a supplement to this book. If the main group does not contain this icon you should create one. To do so, find the ntcmds.hlp file with the File Manager (or use the **File | Search** option to find the file).

IF: The IF command lets you make decisions in a batch file. The command immediately following the condition is executed if the condition is true. That command can be a GOTO command to allow branching and looping. The condition can test for equality between two strings, existence of a file name, or error code values (see Section 7.5.6.5 for an example).

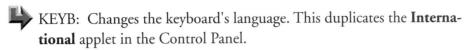 KEYB: Changes the keyboard's language. This duplicates the **International** applet in the Control Panel.

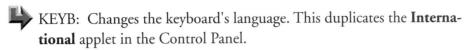 LABEL: Changes the volume label for a drive. This command performs the same function as the **Disk | Change Label** option in the File Manager.

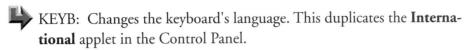 MD, MKDIR: This command creates a new sub-directory in the current directory.

Examples:
mkdir dirname   // creates a new directory in current directory
mkdir a:dirname   // creates a new directory in current directory on A
mkdir ..\dirname   // creates new directory in parent of current directory
mkdir \tmp\dirname // creates a new directory with \tmp as its parent

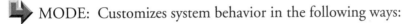 MEM: Displays memory usage.

Examples:
mem   // displays memory usage for MS-DOS system
mem /program   // displays the memory status of loaded programs

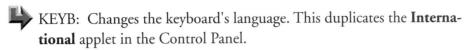 MODE: Customizes system behavior in the following ways:

- printer configuration
- serial port configuration
- device status
- redirecting printer output
- changing the size of the window
- setting keyboard behavior

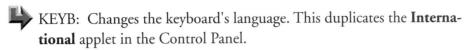 MORE: Combined with other commands using a pipe, the MORE command prints their output one screen at a time. The command can also be used with the "/e" option to emulate the functionality of the UNIX version of MORE. See section 7.5.7.

Examples:
type file1 | more   // displays file1 one screen at a time
more /e file1   // displays file1 one screen at a time
dir | sort | more   // displays output of SORT one screen at a time

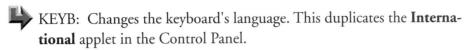 MOVE: Moves files from one directory to another. Files cannot be moved across drives.

Examples:
move file1 file2   // moves file1 to file2–same as RENAME
move file1 ..   // moves file1 to parent of current directory
move file1 \bin\apps // moves file to new directory

PATH: Sets the current path (see Section 7.5.7).

PAUSE: Pauses a batch file and asks the user to press a key to continue (see Section 7.5.6.6 for an example).

POPD: Pops the top directory off the directory stack. See PUSHD.

PRINT: Sends a text file to the default printer (see also MODE).

PROMPT: This command changes the prompt for the command window. The default version shows the current path. Typing PROMPT by itself clears the prompt and replaces it with the drive letter followed by ">" (e.g. - "C>"). You can customize your prompt using the following special symbols as parameters to the PROMPT command:

$q	=
$$	$
$t	time
$d	date
$p	current drive and path
$v	current NT version
$n	drive letter
$g	>
$l	<
$b	|
$_	new line
$e	escape code (code 27)
$h	backspace
all else	taken literally

For example, if you want your prompt to display the current time, date, and path on a two-line prompt, you would use the following command:
prompt Date: $d Time: $t $_$p$g

PUSHD: Pushes the current directory onto a directory stack and changes to a new directory.

Example:
pushd d:\temp

RD: See RMDIR.

RECOVER: This command attempts to recover information from a damaged disk. If a file contains bad sectors, RECOVER can read the remaining valid sectors and piece them together. For text files this technique works well, but almost any other type of file is worthless if even one byte is missing, so the command has its limits.

REM: Used to create comments in batch files.

REN, RENAME: Lets you rename a file. This is the same as the **File | Rename** option in the File Manager.

Examples:
rename file1 file2   // renames file1 as file2
rename a:file1 file2   // renames a:file1 a:file2–no movement

REPLACE: Lets you replace files. For example, if a disk contains a set of files that back up a directory on your hard disk, you can replace the old backup files with the current versions.

RMDIR: This command deletes a directory. The directory must be empty. If the "/s" option is used however, the RMDIR command will remove all files and all sub-directories.

Examples:
rmdir dirname   // removes the directory if it is empty
rmdir /s dirname   // removes the directory and its contents

SET: Sets environment variables. This command performs the same function as the **System** icon in the Control Panel. It can also be used to create variables in batch files (see Section 7.5.5).

SHIFT: This command shifts parameters in batch files (see Section 7.5.6.8 for an example).

SORT: Used with a pipe following another command, the SORT command sorts the text output.

Examples:
type filename | sort   // sorts contents of filename line by line
sort < filename   // same as above
dir | sort   // sorts the current directory

➡ START: executes a program as a separate task, freeing up the command line for use again.

example:
start notepad

➡ TIME: Lets you set the system time. This command performs the same function as the **Date/Time** icon in the Control Panel (see also DATE).

➡ TITLE: Sets the title of the current window.

Example:
title hello   // sets the title of the current window to hello

➡ TREE: This command paints a text version of the directory tree starting at the current directory.

➡ TYPE: Dumps a text file to the screen. Used with MORE to view the file one screen at a time.

Examples:
type file1   // dumps file1 to the screen
type file1 | more   // dumps file1 to screen one screen at a time

➡ VER: Shows the version number for this copy of NT. This command performs the same function as the **Help | About** dialog in the Program Manager.

➡ VERIFY: When this command is ON (e.g., "verify on"), Windows NT verifies that file writes were correctly placed on the disk by rereading each sector after it's written. This slows file writes down a fair amount.

➡ VOL: This command displays the volume label for a drive.

➡ XCOPY: This command is used to copy entire directory trees from one place to another. It is the same as Ctrl-dragging a directory in the directory tree with the File Manager.

NOTEPAD

The Notepad application is a simple text editor. With Notepad you can create batch files (see Section 7.5.5), read existing text files, write programs, type quick notes and README files, and so on.

8.1 Executive Summary

It seems that no matter how sophisticated an operating system gets, there will always be a place for simple text files. In Windows NT you use text files to create batch files, README files, programs, and the like. The Notepad is used to create and read text files. A typical Notepad window is shown in Figure 8.1.

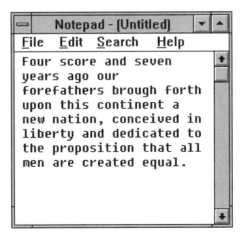

Figure 8.1
The Notepad Application.

The Notepad is a very straightforward text editor. In the File menu you can open and save files, create a new file, print the file, and exit. The Edit menu allows you to cut, copy, paste, and clear selections. You can also select a word wrap option that wraps lines longer than the current window width. The **Time/Date** option inserts the current time and date at the cursor position. Alternately, by placing the string ".LOG" in the first line of a text file, Notepad will automatically append the current time and date to the bottom of that file each time it's loaded. Notepad also contains a search menu that allows you to find a string, or repeat the last find with the F3 key.

If you want a word processor, look at the Write application in Chapter 10. Notepad does little more than read, modify, and write pure ASCII text files.

8.2 Guided Tour

It only takes about five minutes to completely understand the Notepad application because it's so simple. Start it up by double-clicking on the **Notepad** icon in the Accessory group in the Program Manager. As soon as the application is up, you can begin typing in the window. Because you did not ask it to load a file at start-up, Notepad assumes you wish to create a new file.

You can also start Notepad by typing "start notepad" on the command line. If you specify an existing file name on the command line–for example, "start notepad note.txt"–Notepad will open that file and display it.

The File menu contains options to open a file, create a new file, save a file, save a file under a new name, and exit. The Open dialog, shown in Figure 8.2, lets you open an existing file. You can type a file name into the edit area, double-click on a filename in the Files list, or single-click on a file name in the Files list and then click the OK button. You can change directories using the Directories list by double-clicking on the different folder icons. If you get lost, press the Cancel button and start again.

Find a text file and open it. You can move around in it with the scroll bars or the arrow keys. You close a file either by selecting the **New** menu option, opening another file, or exiting.

Select the **New** option from the File menu to create a new file. Create a simple batch file by typing the following lines:

```
@echo off
echo This is a directory listing for the root:
echo.
```

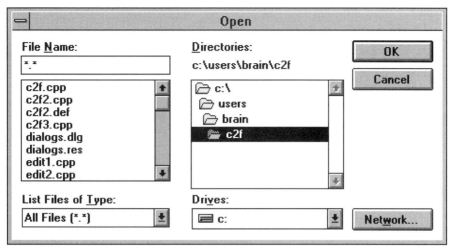

Figure 8.2
The Open dialog.

```
dir \
echo All done.
```

Save this text to a file named `test.bat` by choosing the **File | Save** option and typing the file name (you can also change the save directory by clicking on the directory tree in the Save dialog). If the name `test.bat` already exists in the current directory, you'll see a dialog asking if you want to overwrite the existing file. Answer yes or no. Once the batch file has been saved, you can start a command window by double-clicking on the **MS-DOS** icon in the Main group of the Program Manager. Use the CD command to change to the same directory where Notepad wrote `test.bat` and then type "test" to execute the batch file (see Chapter 7 for more information on Batch files and the MS-DOS window).

If you choose the **Save** option again, Notepad will not prompt you for a file name because it assumes you want to save the file to the same name. If you want to save it to a different name, choose the **Save As** option and you'll be prompted for a new file name.

There are several movement keys defined in Notepad that help you move around the current document with the keyboard. The arrow keys and Page Up and Page Down work as expected. The Home and End keys move to the beginning and end of the current line, while Ctrl-Home and Ctrl-End move to the beginning and end of the document. The scroll bar works as expected.

You can print the file by choosing the **Print** option in the File menu. Before printing, however, look at the **Page Setup** and **Print Setup** options in the File menu. The **Page Setup** option lets you choose the margins for the text on the printed page, as well as the header and footer. The **Print Setup** option lets you change printer settings for the default printer or choose a different printer.

You can select text either by dragging over it or by holding down the Shift key and using the arrow keys, Page Up and Page Down, etc. You can select the entire document using the **Select All** option in the Edit menu.

Once text is selected, you can cut, copy, clear, and paste it to the *Clipboard* with the corresponding commands in the Edit menu. The Clipboard is a memory area shared by all applications. Most applications have access to this area through their Edit menus. Once an application has moved information onto the Clipboard using the **Copy** or **Cut** menu options, that information can be pasted into any other application using the **Paste** option. A given item remains on the clipboard until it's replaced by another item. In Notepad the Clipboard is used in a very simple way. Text strings are copied and pasted from one place in a file to another, or between two different text files. The Guided Tour in Chapter 10 shows much more advanced uses of the Clipboard in Object Linking and Embedding (OLE) applications.

If you do something you did not intend, the **Undo** option in the Edit menu will often let you reverse the last action.

The **Find** option in the Search menu lets you search the current document for a string. Searching starts at the current cursor position and proceeds up or down depending on the setting of the radio box. You can perform case sensitive or insensitive searches.

The Notepad application is very simple, but it does contain a few surprises. The **Time and Date** option in the Edit menu will inject the current time and date at the current cursor position. You can create a log file by typing ".LOG" on the first line of any text file. The next time that file is loaded into Notepad, the time and date will be inserted at the end of the file. The **Word Wrap** option in the Edit menu wraps all lines longer than the current window width.

Exit the application by choosing the **Exit** option in the File menu. If you've made changes to the file that have not yet been saved, you'll see a warning dialog. The Cancel button in this dialog returns you back to the application as if you never requested the **Exit** option.

8.3 Common Questions

? *How do I edit a text file?*
See the Guided Tour of the Notepad application in Section 8.2

? *How do I load a file that does not have an extension into Notepad? It always wants to append ".txt" to it.*
When you type the filename, place a dot at the end of it. For example, to load a file named "makefile," type "makefile." on the command line or in the Open dialog.

? *Can I edit a text file from the command line?*
Yes. Type "notepad filename" or "start notepad filename" where "filename" is the name of the file you wish to load.

? *How do I create a log file in Windows NT?*
Create a text file with the string ".LOG" on the first line. Each time the file is loaded into Notepad, the current time and date will be inserted at the bottom of the file. By creating an icon for the file in the Start-up group, the file will get loaded every time you log in. To do this, Select the **File | New** option in the Program Manager and create a new Program Item. In the Command Line field enter "notepad filename," where "filename" is the name of your log file. In the Working Directory field enter the directory containing the file. Place the icon in the Start-up group in the Program Manager. See Chapter 2.

? *How do I move around the document with the keyboard?*
The arrow keys and Page Up and Page Down work as expected. The Home and End keys move to the beginning and end of the line. The Ctrl-Home and Ctrl-End keys move to the beginning and end of the document.

8.4 Details

8.4.1   The File Menu

The **File** menu allows you to open, save, and print files.

8.4.1.1   The File | New Option

This option clears the current document so you can begin typing a new one. If the current document contains changes that have not yet been saved, you'll see a dialog asking if you want to save them.

8.4.1.2   The File | Open Option

This option lets you open an existing file. You can type a file name or a complete path name into the edit area, or you can type a filter string there to change the contents of the Files list. For example, if you type "*.bat" into the edit area then all the batch files in the current directory will be listed. You can also double-click on a filename in the Files list to open it, or single-click on a file name in the Files list and then click the OK button.

You can change directories using the Directories list. Double-click on the different folder icons to move around and, if you get lost, press the Cancel button and start again (see Figure 8.2).

8.4.1.3   The File | Save Option

This option saves the current document to the file name you gave it when you opened or last saved it. If the current document is a new one, you will see the Save As dialog as described in the next section.

8.4.1.4   The File | Save As Option

This option allows you to save the current document to a new file name. Enter the new name for the file in the edit area and press OK (see Figure 8.3).

8.4.1.5   The File | Print Option

This option prints the file to the default printer. Change the default printer with the **Print Setup** option or in the Printer Manager.

8.4.1.6   The File | Page Setup Option

This option lets you change the margins and the header and footer for the document (see Figure 8.4).

8.4.1.7   The File | Print Setup Option

This option displays a standard printer setup dialog that allows you to change the default printer and select from its options (see Figure 8.5).

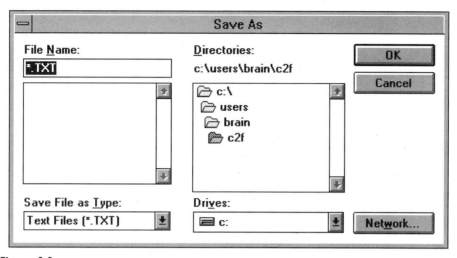

Figure 8.3
The Save As dialog.

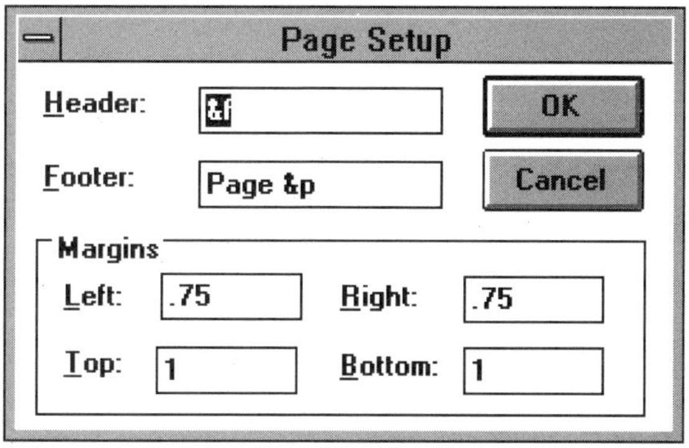

Figure 8.4
The Page Setup dialog.

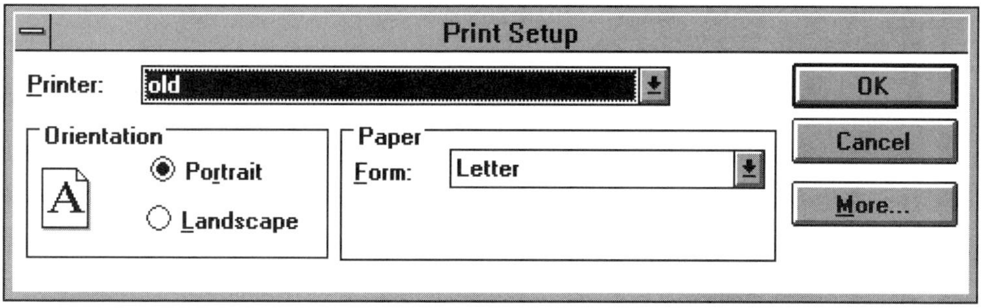

Figure 8.5
The Print Setup dialog.

8.4.1.8   The File | Exit Option

This option terminates the Notepad application. If changes have not been saved you'll see a dialog warning you of this fact.

8.4.2   The Edit Menu

The Edit menu manipulates the Clipboard (see the Guided Tour for a description) and the document.

8.4.2.1   The Edit | Undo Option

The **Undo** option undoes the last change you made to the document.

8.4.2.2   The Edit | Cut Option

This option is only available if you've selected a piece of text in the document by dragging over it with the mouse. It deletes the selected text and places it on the Clipboard. That text can then be pasted elsewhere in the current document, or in a different document.

8.4.2.3   The Edit | Copy Option

This option is only available if you've selected a piece of text in the document by dragging over it with the mouse. It copies the selected text and places it on the Clipboard. That text can then be pasted elsewhere in the current document, or in a different document.

8.4.2.4   The Edit | Paste Option

This option is available only if the Clipboard contains text that can be pasted into this document. The text on the Clipboard is copied into the document at the current insertion point.

8.4.2.5   The Edit | Delete Option

This option is only available if you've selected a piece of text in the document by dragging over it with the mouse. The selected text is deleted. The Delete key does the same.

8.4.2.6   The Edit | Select All Option

This option selects all text in the current document. It's the same as dragging the mouse over the entire document.

8.4.2.7   The Edit | Time/Date Option

This option inserts the current time and date into the document at the insertion point. If you place the word ".LOG" on the first line of the document, the current time and date will be automatically appended to the file whenever it's loaded into Notepad.

8.4.2.8   The Edit | Word Wrap Option

This option causes long lines to be wrapped within the boundaries of the current window.

8.4.3   The Search Menu

This menu lets you find text strings in the current document.

8.4.3.1   The Search | Find Option

This option presents a dialog that allows you to enter the search string. Searching starts at the current cursor position and proceeds up or down depending on the setting of the radio box. Searching stops at the end or beginning of the document, depending on the direction (see Figure 8.6).

8.4.3.2   The Search | Find Next Option

This option repeats the last search from the current cursor position. Pressing F3 does the same thing.

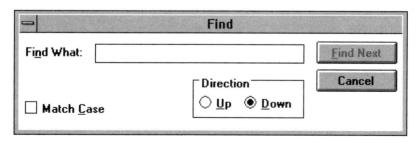

Figure 8.6
The Search dialog.

PAINTBRUSH

One of the biggest reasons for using a GUI is the ability to create and display graphical images. The Paintbrush application lets you create bitmap images and also lets you access and edit screen dumps.

9.1 Executive Summary

Paintbrush creates and edits bitmapped images. A bitmapped image is made up of fixed-size and fixed-resolution pixels. This characteristic distinguishes it from a drawing, which is made up of stroked lines. (Windows NT does not ship with a drawing editor, but most applications that could use one, like Microsoft Word, Microsoft Works, etc., include a drawing editor that works in a manner very similar to the Paintbrush application). One of the most common uses of Paintbrush is to capture and edit screen dumps.

Paintbrush is fairly sophisticated and it contains all the tools you'd expect to find. You can draw lines, rectangles, and circles, as well as bezier curves. You can flood fill and erase either selectively or completely. You can also select areas of the painting and cut or copy it to the Clipboard. Paintbrush is an OLE server, so you can link or embed anything you copy to the Clipboard and then insert it in other applications like the Write word processor discussed in Chapter 10. You can also flip, invert, re-size, or tilt the selected area to create interesting effects. The **Option** menu lets you create color palettes, set the size of the painting, change brush shapes, and so on.

If you press the PrtSc (print screen) or Alt-PrtSc buttons, the entire screen or the current window, respectively, will be dumped to the Clipboard. You can then paste the image into Paintbrush and edit it. For example, we used this capability to create Figure 9.1, which shows a typical view of the Paintbrush application in action. All the screen dumps in this book were created using Paintbrush.

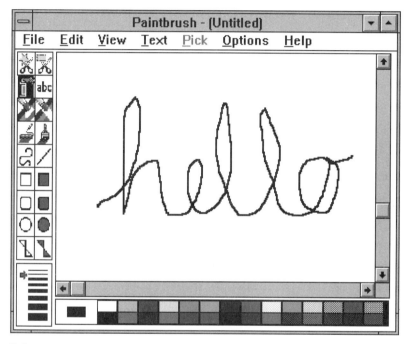

Figure 9.1
The Paintbrush application.

9.2 Guided Tour

Open up the Paintbrush application by double-clicking on its icon in the Accessories group of the Program Manager. There is a Toolbox on the left-hand side of the screen. Find the brush icon in the Toolbox and click on it. Move the cursor out into the drawing area and drag it around. You are now drawing. In the **Options** menu the **Brush Shapes** dialog allows you to change the shape of the brush. Try several different brushes and see what they do. You can also change the brush width using the Selection tool in the bottom left corner of the Paintbrush window.

Using the Brush tool, draw a closed figure. For example, draw a dog bone shape. Now choose the tool that looks like a paint roller. This tool is the Flood Fill tool. The hot spot is located at the bottom left side of the cursor at the point of the triangle. Click it inside your dog bone and, provided there are no holes in its border, the inside of the bone will fill with the current color. Choose the **Undo** option in the Edit menu to undo the fill.

Move toward the bottom of the screen and click on a different color in the Color Palette. Notice the rectangle on the left side of the Palette changes to record your current selection. Now fill the dog bone again with the new color. Clicking on a color in the Color Palette chooses it for the current brush color. Clicking on a color with the right mouse button chooses a Pen color. If you look in the Toolbar there are two rectangle icons, two circle icons, two polygon icons, and two rounded rectangle icons. The left version is unfilled, while the right version is filled. Try changing the two colors in the Palette and then drawing a filled rectangle. To draw a rectangle, choose the icon, click on the upper left corner of the rectangle, and then drag to the lower right corner. The rectangle's border will be painted in the current Pen color, while the inside will be filled with the current Brush color.

You can create text by clicking on the icon containing the letters "abc" and then clicking in the drawing area at the appropriate insertion point for the text. You can change the font using the **Fonts** option in the Text menu.

There are two Erasers in the tool box. The right-hand one erases everything in its path and replaces it with the color chosen with the right mouse button. The left-hand one erases only the color chosen from the Color Palette with the left-hand mouse button. Create a drawing with several colors and try out the two different Erasers. Double-clicking on the eraser icon applies it globally.

The two Scissors tools in the Toolbox allow you to select portions of the painting. Using the rectangular selector you can select any rectangular portion of the painting. The other selector lets you select any shape you like. Once you've selected part of the drawing you can move the selection by dragging it, or copy the selection by Ctrl-dragging it. Cut or copy the selection to the Clipboard with the appropriate options in the Clipboard menu. You can also paste from the Clipboard and then move it around. You can manipulate the current selection with the Pick menu. For example, you can flip the selection, invert it, shrink or grow it, and so on. Try out these different options.

The View menu lets you change your view of the drawing. For example, you can zoom in to manipulate individual bits, or zoom out to see the whole drawing. You can also control whether or not the Toolbox and Color Palette are visible. By choosing the **Cursor Position** option you can create a small window that tells you where the cursor is.

Press the PrtSc key. This will copy the contents of the current screen to the Clipboard. You can then paste the screen dump into the current painting using the **Paste** option in the Edit menu. Alt-PrtSc will dump the current window, rather than the entire screen, to the Clipboard. Paste it the same way.

To print the current painting select the **Print** option in the File menu. **Page Setup** allows you to modify margins and create a header or footer.

9.3 Common Questions

How do I combine text and paintings in a document?
See Chapter 10.

How do I insert a screen dump into a document?
Use the PrtSc (print screen) or Alt-PrtSc key to copy the current screen or window to the Clipboard. Paste it into the Paintbrush application. Use the Selection tool to select the portion you want and copy it to the Clipboard.

When you talk about the "Toolbox" and "Color Palette" it makes no sense to me. Where are they?
By default the Toolbox and Color Palette are displayed, but if someone has changed your defaults then one or both may be invisible. Click on the **Tools and Linesize** or **Palette** options in the View menu to make these objects visible.

How do I change brush shape?
The width of the brush is changed using the tool in the lower left corner of the window. The shape is changed using the **Brush Shape** option in the Options menu.

The drawing area is very small even though the application window is large. How do I fix that?
Go to the **Image Attributes** option in the Options menu and change the image size.

9.4 Details

9.4.1   The File Menu

The File Menu lets you open, save, and print bitmap files.

9.4.1.1   The File | New Option

This option creates a new bitmap file. If the current file contains changes that have not been saved, you'll see a warning that asks if you want to save the changes first. The size of the new painting is controlled by the size specified in the **Image Attributes** option of the Options menu.

9.4.1.2   The File | Open Option

This option lets you open an existing file. You can type a file name or a complete path name into the edit area, or you can type a filter string there to change the contents of the Files list. You can double-click on a file name in the Files list to open it, or single-click and then click the OK button.

You can change directories using the Directories list. Double-click on the different folder icons to move around and, if you get lost, press the Cancel button and start again (see Figure 9.2).

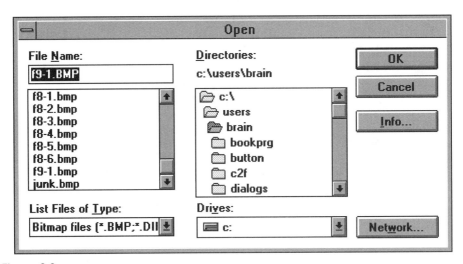

Figure 9.2
The Open dialog.

9.4.1.3   The File | Save Option

This options saves the file to the current file name. If it's a new file, the Save As dialog will appear to get the new file name.

9.4.1.4   The File | Save As Option

This option presents a dialog that allows you to save the current file to a new name. Type the new name in the edit field.

9.4.1.5   The File | Print Option

This option prints the document on the default printer. If the image is larger than will fit on a single page (see Section 9.4.6.6), the image will be printed on several sheets.

9.4.1.6   The File | Print Setup Option

This option lets you choose the default printer and customize its behavior.

9.4.1.7   The File | Page Setup Option

This option lets you change margins and the header and footer on the printed page (see Figure 9.3).

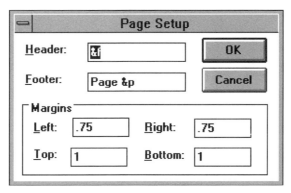

Figure 9.3
The Page Setup dialog.

9.4.1.8   The File | Exit Option

This option terminates the Paintbrush application. If changes have not been saved, a dialog warns of the problem before exiting.

9.4.2   The Edit Menu

This menu gives you access to the Clipboard. Paintbrush is an OLE server, so anything it places on the Clipboard can be embedded. If the file has been saved, anything it places on the Clipboard can also be linked.

9.4.2.1   The Edit | Undo Option

This option undoes the last change. Anything you draw with a single drag, no matter how large, can be undone. Once you begin another drag, however, the previous change is permanent. In a paint program there is no way to select and delete an object because the painting consists only of pixels, not objects. You can use an eraser to erase it, but that's all.

9.4.2.2   The Edit | Cut Option

This option cuts the current selection to the Clipboard. Select part or all of the drawing with one of the two Scissors tools in the Toolbox. See Chapter 10 for a discussion of how to use the clipboard.

9.4.2.3   The Edit | Copy Option

This option copies the current selection to the Clipboard. Select part or all of the drawing with one of the two Scissors tools in the Toolbox. See Chapter 10 for a discussion of how to use the clipboard.

9.4.2.4   The Edit | Paste Option

This option pastes the contents of the Clipboard into the current drawing. The pasted piece will be selected, so you can move it into position by dragging it.

9.4.2.5   The Edit | Copy To Option

This option copies the selected portion of the drawing to a new file. You'll see a dialog similar to the Save As dialog that allows you to specify a new file name.

9.4.2.6   The Edit | Paste From Option

This option allows you to paste from a file on disk. A dialog similar to the Open dialog will appear so you can select the file.

9.4.3   The View Menu

This menu lets you change your perspective on the current painting by zooming, and by adding and removing tools.

9.4.3.1   The View | Zoom In Option

The **Zoom In** option lets you zoom in and manipulate your painting pixel-by-pixel. When you select the option a rectangle appears. Move it to select that portion of the image you want to modify. You'll see a grid as shown in Figure 9.4. Clicking on the grid with the left mouse button paints the selected pixel with the palette color chosen by the left mouse button, and clicking on the grid with the right mouse button paints the selected pixel with the color chosen by the right button. The upper left portion of the window displays an actual-size view of the pixels you're changing. You can click in this area to access the pixels underneath it.

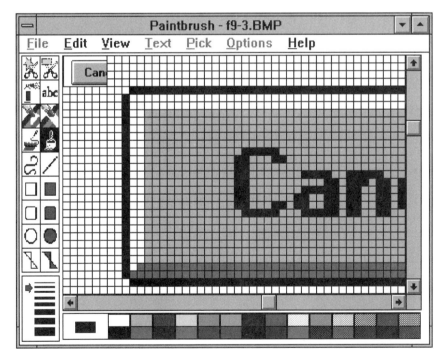

Figure 9.4
The Zoom In screen.

9.4.3.2   The View | Zoom Out Option

The **Zoom Out** option lets you view the entire drawing scaled to a single screen. You cannot draw in this mode, but you can use the Scissors tools to select portions of the drawing you wish to copy to the Clipboard.

9.4.3.3   The View | Tools and Linesize Option

This option lets you enable and disable the Toolbox and the Linesize box from the display. Disabling the Toolbox lets you see more of your drawing on the screen at once. Re-select the option to bring the Toolbox back.

9.4.3.4   The View | Palette Option

This option lets you enable and disable the Color Palette from the display. Disabling the Palette lets you see more of your drawing on the screen at once. Re-select the option to bring the Palette back.

9.4.3.5   The View | Cursor Position Option

This option creates a very small window that continuously displays the current position of your cursor. You can move this small window, although Paintbrush will not let you move it over any part of the actual drawing (see Figure 9.5).

Figure 9.5
The Cursor Position window.

9.4.4   The Text Menu

The Text menu lets you customize the appearance of text that you draw.

9.4.4.1   The Text | Regular Option

This option clears the **Bold**, **Italic**, **Underline**, **Shadow**, and **Outline** options.

9.4.4.2   The Text | Bold Option

This option can be toggled on and off. When it's on it causes all text subsequently created to appear in **boldface**.

9.4.4.3   The Text | Italic Option

This option can be toggled on and off. When it's on it causes all text subsequently created to appear in *italics*.

9.4.4.4   The Text | Underline Option

This option can be toggled on and off. When it's on it causes all text subsequently created to appear <u>underlined</u>.

9.4.4.5   The Text | Outline Option

This option can be toggled on and off. When it's on it causes all text subsequently created to appear outlined. This option and the following option are mutually exclusive.

9.4.4.6   The Text | Shadow Option

This option can be toggled on and off. When it's on it causes all text subsequently created to appear shadowed. This option and the previous option are mutually exclusive.

9.4.4.7   The Text | Fonts Option

This option allows you to select a different font using the standard font selection dialog as shown in Figure 9.6. You can select the font, the style and the size, and see a sample in the Sample area.

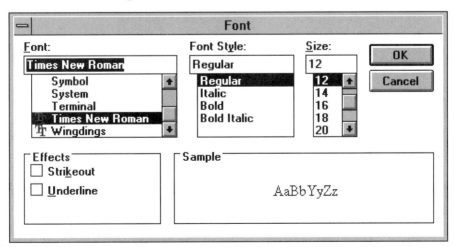

Figure 9.6
The Font dialog.

9.4.5   The Pick Menu

Once you select a portion of the drawing with the Scissors tool, you can manipulate the selected piece with the Pick menu.

9.4.5.1   The Pick | Flip Horizontal Option

This option flips the selected pixels across a horizontal axis.

9.4.5.2   The Pick | Flip Vertical Option

This option flips the selected pixels across a vertical axis.

9.4.5.3   The Pick | Inverse Option

This option chromatically inverts the colors of the selected pixels. Black becomes white, white becomes black, yellow becomes blue, and so on. Re-inverting returns the colors back to the way they started.

9.4.5.4   The Pick | Shrink and Grow Option

This option lets you shrink or grow a selected portion of the drawing. Select part of the drawing. Click this option. Now drag out a new rectangle. The selected portion of the text will be reduced or enlarged to fit in that rectangle. You can shrink and grow the originally selected area many times by dragging new rectangles. The system remembers the original selection. Click on this option again when you're done.

9.4.5.5   The Pick | Tilt Option

This option works like the previous option but it tilts the copy made. Select a part of the drawing with the Scissors tool. Select the **Tilt** option. Click on the drawing and drag to tilt the rectangle.

9.4.5.6   The Pick | Clear Option

If this option is selected then the originally selected part of the drawing is cleared before each **Tile** or **Shrink and Grow** operation.

9.4.6   The Options Menu

This menu lets you customize the Paintbrush program.

9.4.6.1 The Options I Image Attributes Option

This option lets you select the size of the image. You can also specify whether the drawing will be black and white or color. You can make the image very large, but the number of pixels that must be stored in memory and on disk grows with image size (for example, an image that is 40 inches high requires 5,000 pixels in the Y direction, so a 40" by 40" image would require 25 megabytes of memory). On very large images, you can use extremely large fonts, 500 points for example, (see Figure 9.7).

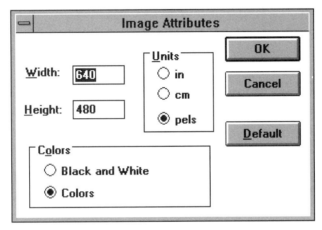

Figure 9.7
The Image Attributes dialog.

9.4.6.2 The Options I Brush Shapes Option

This option lets you choose different brush shapes so you can create different effects, draw calligraphy, and so on (see Figure 9.8).

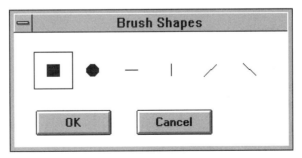

Figure 9.8
The Brush Shapes dialog.

9.4.6.3   The Options | Edit Colors Option

This option lets you edit the colors in the Palette. Select one of the colors with the left mouse button and then choose this option. Create a new color. When you press the OK button the selected color in the Palette will change.

9.4.6.4   The Options | Get Colors Option

This option lets you retrieve a Palette you stored on disk with the following option.

9.4.6.5   The Options | Save Colors Attributes Option

This option lets you store a Palette on disk for future use.

9.4.6.6   The Options | Omit Picture Format Option

When the Paintbrush application stores information on the Clipboard, it stores it in two different formats. By selecting this option you eliminate the Picture format and thereby reduce the memory space and time associated with having two formats on the clipboard.

W̄RITE

The Notepad application is fine for creating batch files and other simple text files where pure ASCII text output is desirable, but you wouldn't want to use it to create a report for your boss. The Write application, on the other hand, is a complete word processor. In this chapter you will learn how to use the Write application to create professional documents.

10.1 Executive Summary

Write is a complete word processor that lets you create professional documents. Figure 10.1 shows you a typical Write screen while editing a document.

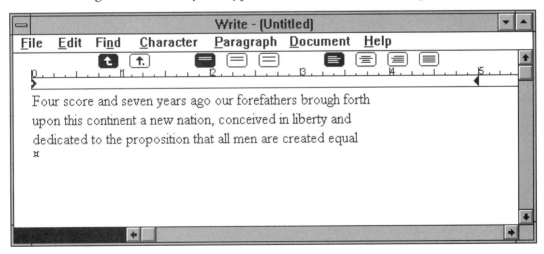

Figure 10.1
The Write application.

The following list identifies many of the features available in the Write application:

- Multiple fonts, multiple text sizes, italics, boldface, superscripts, and subscripts
- Center, left, or right-justified text
- Tabbed formatting for tables and lists
- Single, one-and-a-half, or double spacing
- Embedded and linked figures from the Paintbrush application (see Chapter 9)
- Headers and footers
- A ruler that helps lay out tabs, margins, and spacing

Write can create a wide variety of documents–letters, reports, flyers, and so on–that look extremely professional.

One of the nicest things about Write is that Microsoft made it compatible with its higher-level products. For example, both Microsoft Works and Microsoft Word use the same control characters for cut, copy, paste, bold, italics, and underline. Both of the higher-level products can also accept Write documents and translate them automatically. Learning to use Write therefore accelerates your ability to learn other word processors. The time you spend is not wasted.

Write is an OLE application. See the Guided Tour in Section 10.2 for a description of the different OLE modes.

10.2 Guided Tour

Probably the best way to learn how to use the Write word processor is to create a document with it. In this Guided Tour you'll walk through the process of recreating the first two pages of this chapter. However, if you have a report you need to create for a committee meeting tomorrow morning, start with it and use the formatting principles discussed in this tour to spruce up its appearance.

There are two distinct phases to writing with a word processor: typing and formatting. Typing gets the characters that make up the document into the system. Formatting makes those characters appear pleasing to the human eye. Some tend to type and then format in two distinct phases, while others prefer to format as they go along. You will find a style that works best for you.

Let's say you want to recreate the first page or two of this chapter in Write. These two pages offer a good example document because they contain several different fonts, a picture, and a variety of formatting techniques. Start by typing in the text. We'll come back and format it later. In the case of the chapter title, section headings, captions, and other elements that do not fill a complete line, press return at the end of each line. In the case of paragraphs, type until you reach the end of each paragraph and then press return. The system will automatically word wrap. If you have the patience, type in the first two pages of this chapter. If not, type in little bits and pieces to simulate the contents of the first two pages.

Now let's work through the text and format it. Start by moving the mouse toward the left edge of the window until it changes from an I-beam into an arrow pointing to the upper right. Hold down the Control key on the keyboard and click. This will select the entire document. Choose the **Fonts** option in the Character menu and pick the Times New Roman font in size 12 (12 points). This is the closest approximation of the book's text font, and using it across the entire document like this will save a lot of formatting time later. Press the OK button and the entire document changes to this new font. Now start at the top of the document and select the chapter title and number. Drag over them with the mouse to select them. We need a large font for these characters to match the chapter title in the book. Select the **Fonts** option at the bottom of the Character menu and click on several font names and sizes until you find a font that's close in appearance and size to the one in this book. When you press the OK button, the selected text will pick up the new font. If it doesn't look right in the document, try again. You can use the **Reduce Font** and **Enlarge Font** options in the Character menu to bump the size up or down a bit.

The first letter of this chapter's text is larger. To recreate this effect, select the first character and then pick a larger font for it in the Font menu. Bump the size up and down until you like what you see.

Choose the **Ruler On** option in the Document menu and watch what happens. A formatting aid called the *ruler* appears, as shown in Figure 10.2. This ruler is extremely handy for setting tabs, margins, and spacing. Look for a small triangle on the left side of the ruler. It marks the left margin. Sitting on top of it is a very small square. You can drag the square, so move it toward the middle of the ruler. When you drop it, the first line of the paragraph will indent to the square. The change you made on the ruler applies *only to the selected text*. Insert a tab to tab over the chapter number by clicking below the ruler. If you want to recreate the line and reverse-video, you can do it in Paintbrush. See below.

Figure 10.2
The Ruler in Write.

Now format the heading for Section 10.1. Select the heading and choose a font for it. You may also want to choose the **Bold** option in the Character menu (or in the Font dialog) to make this text boldface. You can convert text to italics or underlined in the same way. Select it, then choose the appropriate menu option from the Character menu.

You can format normal paragraphs (the first paragraph is not normal) in either of two ways. You can create the indentation using the technique shown for the ruler bar or you can press the Tab key to indent. If you do not like the tab distance, you can select a group of lines and then click in the same area where the margin triangles are located. Either a normal tab or a decimal tab will be created at the clicked location depending on which of the two **Tab** buttons is highlighted. Once you've created a tab you can drag it. This technique is extremely useful for creating tables. You can space out the tabs and decimal tabs to format words and numbers in the table.

Eventually you'll come to Figure 10.1. To capture it, first hold down the Alt key and press the PrtSc (print screen) key. This will dump a copy of your Write window into the Clipboard. You can, if you choose, simply paste the image directly into the document. This technique has the advantage of simplicity but the disadvantage of inflexibility. There is no way to edit the screen dump once it's pasted into the document. Because this is an OLE client application, and because the Paintbrush application is an OLE server, two other techniques are available: *embedding* and *linking*.

Let's try embedding first. Start up the Paintbrush application (see Chapter 9) and paste the screen dump there. The screen dump will already be selected after the paste (or use the rectangular Scissors tool to select a portion of the painting). Copy it to the Clipboard and then paste it into the Write document with the normal **Paste** option in the Edit menu. This is an *embedded* figure.

Since it was copied from the Paintbrush application, you can double-click on it in your write document to edit. The Paintbrush application will automatically start up and display the figure. Once you've changed it, choose the **Up-date** option and the figure will be modified in the document automatically.

It is also possible to *link* a figure that exists on the disk. Using this technique, several documents can *share* the same figure. Any change to the original figure is immediately reflected in all documents linked to it. To try out this capability, save your screen dump to a file using the Paintbrush application. Copy the screen dump from Paintbrush to the Clipboard and then, in Write, choose the **Paste Special** option in the Edit menu. Click the **Paste Link** button. You can then paste a link into several other locations or documents if you like. Now if you change the originating Paintbrush file, all linked images will change accordingly.

The differences between the three pasting options are summarized below:

- A straight copy of the screen dump from the Clipboard pastes an unchangeable image into the document. The only way to change it is to delete it and re-paste.
- Pasting the screen dump into the Paintbrush application and then copying from there and doing a normal Paste into the document embeds the figure. You can edit the figure by double-clicking on it. Any changes are local to that one figure.
- Saving the screen dump to a file with the Paintbrush application, copying some or all of the figure from that file, and then using the **Paste Special** option to form a link creates a figure that can be shared by many different documents. Any change to the original file is reflected in all documents linked to it.

The OLE techniques described above are used by many Windows NT applications to provide improved Clipboard flexibility.

You can re-size or move the figure by Choosing the **Move Picture** and **Size Picture** options in the Edit menu. Once the cursor changes after selecting **Move Picture**, horizontal cursor movements reposition the figure. No clicking or dragging is required until you reach the final destination. Once there, you click to end repositioning and return the cursor to normal. Once the cursor changes after selecting **Size Picture**, move the cursor toward a border without clicking or dragging. When you touch a border, the border will move with the cursor until you click to end the move. If you make a mistake, the **Undo** option in the Edit menu is always available.

The final touches needed in this document are proper margins, page numbers, and a header. Choose the **Page Layout** option in the Document menu to select margins and the starting page number. To create a header for the document, choose the **Header** option in the **Document** menu. You'll be shown a blank page in which to create the header. The dialog is modeless. That is, you can type on the blank page while the dialog is on the screen. Click on the **Page Number** button and then type in any text you'd like to have in the header as well. Return to the document when you are finished. The header will appear when you print the document.

Play with several of the other menu options while you're here. For example, double-space a paragraph by selecting it and choosing the **Double Space** option in the Paragraph menu (or use the appropriate button on the ruler). Also try different justifications. The ruler has buttons that do the same things.

When you're ready to print, choose the **Print Setup** option to set up your printer and then print the document.

10.3 Common Questions

How do I change the font on a section of text?
Select the text by dragging over it, and choose the **Fonts** option in the Character menu. There are many other easy-to-use options in the Character menu that let you fine-tune the appearance of text.

How do I center the title of my paper?
Select the title with the mouse and then use the **Center** option in the Paragraph menu.

How do I double-space my report?
Select the entire document and choose the **Double Space** option in the Paragraph menu.

I want to single-space a quotation and move its margins in a little. How do I do that?
See Question 5 to display the ruler. Select the quotation by dragging over it with the mouse. Move the two small triangles on the ruler inward to

constrict the margins. Then, click on the **Single Space** button on the ruler or select that option from the Paragraph menu.

There must be an easier way to set tabs, margins, and the like besides using the menu options. What is it?
Display the ruler by selecting the **Ruler On** option in the Document menu. The ruler gives you a graphical way to set all the common formatting options like tabs, margins, line spacing, etc. Select a section of the text and modify the ruler. The changes will apply only to the selection.

What is the difference between an embedded figure, a copied figure, and a linked figure?
See the description in the Guided Tour in Section 10.2.

What is the quickest way to change the attributes on a piece of text. How do you underline something, for example?
Select it and type Ctrl-U. See the Character menu and look for other accelerators like Ctrl-U next to the menu options.

10.4 Details

10.4.1   The File Menu

The File menu lets you open, save, and print a file.

10.4.1.1   The File | New Option

This option creates a new document. If the previous document hasn't been saved then you'll see a dialog that advises you of the unsaved changes.

10.4.1.2   The File | Open Option

This option lets you open an existing file. You can type a file name or a complete path name into the edit area, or you can type a filter string there to change the contents of the Files list. You can double-click on a file name in the Files list to open it, or single-click on a file name in the Files list and then click the OK button.

You can change directories using the Directories list. Double-click on the different folder icons to move around and, if you get lost, press the Cancel button and start again.

10.4.1.3   The File | Save Option

This option saves the document to the current file name. If it's a new document the Save As dialog will appear.

10.4.1.4   The File | Save As Option

This option allows you to save the document under a new file name. The dialog that appears allows you to enter the new name and change the directory or drive.

10.4.1.5   The File | Print Option

This option prints the document on the default printer. You can specify a page range or you can print the entire document. You can also request multiple copies.

10.4.1.6   The File | Print Setup Option

This option lets you select the printer and adjust its behavior.

10.4.1.7   The File | Repaginate Option

This option repaginates the entire file so page breaks are calculated accurately.

10.4.1.8   The File | Exit Option

This option terminates the Write application. If changes have not been saved, then a dialog warns of the problem before exiting.

10.4.2   The Edit Menu

This menu gives you access to the Clipboard. Since Write is an OLE client, it can embed or link from other OLE servers such as Paintbrush.

10.4.2.1   The Edit | Undo Option

This option undoes the previous action.

10.4.2.2   The Edit | Cut Option

This option cuts the currently selected portion of the document to the Clipboard. The selection can then be pasted into other documents.

10.4.2.3   The Edit | Copy Option

This option copies the currently selected portion of the document to the Clipboard. The selection can then be pasted into other documents.

10.4.2.4   The Edit | Paste Option

This option pastes the contents of the Clipboard into the current document. If the Clipboard entry was placed there by an OLE server, then the object will be embedded (and can be edited by double-clicking on it in the document). If not, it will simply be pasted.

10.4.2.5   The Edit | Paste Special Option

This option is only available if the current selection on the Clipboard was placed there by an OLE server such as Paintbrush (see Chapter 9). You will see the dialog shown in Figure 10.3 when you select the option. This dialog shows the source, the different formats in which the data was placed on the Clipboard, and several buttons. Use the default format. If you click on the **Paste** button the selection is embedded (this button is equivalent to the **Paste** option in the Edit menu). If you click on the **Paste Link** button the selection is linked (see the Guided Tour in section 10.2 for a description of the differences and an example).

If the **Paste Link** button is not available, it generally means that the file hasn't been saved yet in the OLE server. Save the file in the server and recopy the selection to the Clipboard.

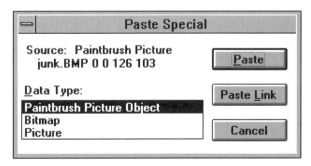

Figure 10.3
Paste Special dialog.

10.4.2.6   The Edit | Links Option

This option displays all the links in the current file and lets you customize them. For example, you can specify whether links are updated automatically or manually.

10.4.2.7   The Edit | Edit ... Object Option

This option lets you edit a linked or embedded object in the application from which it came. If the object is embedded, you'll see the object itself in its application. If it's linked, the application will bring up the file from which it's linked in the application. An alternate method is to double-click on the object.

10.4.2.8   The Edit | Insert Object Option

This option allows you to insert a new object of the specified type. The appropriate application will execute and you can create the new object in it.

10.4.2.9   The Edit | Move Picture Option

This option allows you to move a picture that has been previously pasted into the document. Select the picture you want to move, then select the menu option. The cursor will change and any horizontal mouse movement will reposition the drawing (you do not need to drag–just move the mouse from side to side). Click on the final destination (see also the **Left**, **Centered**, and **Right** options in the Paragraph menu).

10.4.2.10   The Edit | Size Picture Option

This option allows you to re-size a figure pasted from another application. Click on the figure. Move the mouse (do not drag it) toward a border. Once the cursor hits one of the borders it begins to move with the mouse. Click at the final size.

10.4.3   The Find Menu

This menu lets you find and replace text in the document.

10.4.3.1   The Find | Find Option

This option lets you find a string in the document. Enter the string and click on the **Find Next** button. The search begins at the current cursor position and moves down.

10.4.3.2   The Find | Repeat Last Find Option

This option repeats the last find.

10.4.3.3   The Find | Replace Option

This option presents a dialog where you type the string you're looking for and the new string that will replace it. Click the **Find Next** button to find the string and the **Replace** button to replace it. **Replace All** replaces all occurrences of the old string.

10.4.3.4   The Find | Go to Page Option

This option presents a dialog that allows you to enter a page number that you can jump to in the document.

10.4.4   The Character Menu

This menu lets you adjust the appearance of characters in your document.

10.4.4.1   The Character | Regular Option

This option returns the selected text to its normal state–no underlining, no boldfacing, etc.

10.4.4.2   The Character | Bold Option

This option changes the selected text to boldface. If you select this option and no text is selected, then anything you type at that insertion point will appear in boldface.

10.4.4.3   The Character | Italic Option

This option changes the selected text to italics. If you select this option and no text is selected, then anything you type at that insertion point will appear in italics.

10.4.4.4   The Character | Underline Option

This option changes the selected text to underlined. If you select this option and no text is selected, then anything you type at that insertion point will appear underlined.

10.4.4.5   The Character | Superscript Option

This option changes the selected text to superscript. If you select this option and no text is selected, then anything you type at that insertion point will appear as superscript.

10.4.4.6   The Character | Subscript Option

This option changes the selected text to subscript. If you select this option and no text is selected, then anything you type at that insertion point will appear as subscript.

10.4.4.7   The Character | Reduce Font Option

This option reduces the font size of the selected text one notch.

10.4.4.8   The Character | Enlarge Font Option

This option increases the font size of the selected text one notch.

10.4.4.9   The Character | Fonts Option

This option presents a dialog that allows you to change the font, style, and size of the currently selected text. If no text is selected, the font will apply to everything subsequently typed at that insertion point.

10.4.5   The Paragraph Menu

This menu allows you to customize the look of a paragraph.

10.4.5.1   The Paragraph | Normal Option

This option returns the selected paragraph to "normal," which is left-justified and single-spaced.

10.4.5.2   The Paragraph | Left Option

This option changes the selected text to left justification.

10.4.5.3   The Paragraph | Centered Option

This option changes the selected text to center justification.

10.4.5.4   The Paragraph | Right Option

This option changes the selected text to right justification.

10.4.5.5   The Paragraph | Justified Option

This option causes all text in the selected paragraphs to be justified at both margins, so it appears flush to the margin on both sides of the paragraph.

10.4.5.6   The Paragraph | Single Space Option

This option single-spaces the selected paragraphs.

10.4.5.7   The Paragraph | 1 and 1/2 Space Option

This option spaces the selected paragraphs with a half-space between lines.

10.4.5.8   The Paragraph | Double Space Option

This option double-spaces the selected paragraphs.

10.4.5.9   The Paragraph | Indent Option

This option allows you to set left, right, and first line indentations from a dialog. It's generally much easier to do it from the ruler (see the Guided Tour in Section 10.2 for an example).

10.4.6   The Document Menu

This menu lets you customize the appearance of a document.

10.4.6.1   The Document | Header Option

10.4.6.2   The Document | Footer Option

These two options let you create headers and footers. Select the option and you'll see a new screen and dialog. It appears as though the document has been completely erased but it hasn't. The new screen is simply the space you use to enter the header or footer. The dialog that appears is modeless, so you can type in the editing area while the dialog is on screen. If it's in the way, move it.

Type the header or footer text in the edit area. Most of the menu options work and allow you to format the text. Insert a page number with the appropriate button in the dialog if you like.

The Distance from Top field lets you adjust the distance of the header or footer from the top or bottom of the page. You'll want to make sure that this distance and the top and bottom margins do not conflict.

10.4.6.3   The Document | Ruler On/Off Option

This option turns the formatting ruler on and off (see the Guided Tour in Section 10.2 for an example).

10.4.6.4   The Document | Tabs Option

This option lets you set tabs for the selected portion of the document. It's much easier to do this with the ruler (see the Guided Tour in Section 10.2 for an example).

10.4.6.5   The Document | Page Layout Option

This option lets you set the margins and starting page number for the document.

TERMINAL

If you have a modem connected to your workstation, you can use the Terminal application to communicate with bulletin board systems and other computers. Terminal offers all the basic services you need to dial into the machine, communicate with it, and download files.

11.1 Executive Summary

The Terminal application is a basic communications package that contains all the services you need to dial up remote computers and bulletin board systems and communicate with them. Figure 11.1 shows a typical session with the Terminal application.

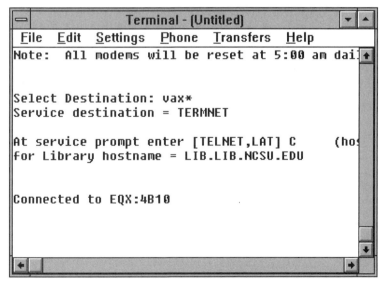

```
Terminal - (Untitled)
 File   Edit   Settings   Phone   Transfers   Help
Note:   All modems will be reset at 5:00 am dai

Select Destination: vax*
Service destination = TERMNET

At service prompt enter [TELNET,LAT] C      (hos
for Library hostname = LIB.LIB.NCSU.EDU


Connected to EQX:4B10
```

Figure 11.1
The Terminal application.

Terminal contains terminal emulators for VT-100, VT-52, and TTY terminals. Terminal also has basic uploading and downloading facilities for text and binary files using the XModem or Kermit protocols. It automatically handles the modem commands when you dial a number and when you hang up. You can change modem commands and terminal settings using the Settings menu.

11.2 Guided Tour

Start the Terminal application by double-clicking on its icon in the Accessories group of the Program Manager. The application will open with a blank screen. If you've never used the Terminal application, it may display a dialog requesting you to choose from the available COM ports. Pick the port to which your modem is connected.

In the Settings menu choose the **Communications** option. It displays a dialog that lets you change the COM port and set communications parameters such as baud rate and parity (see Figure 11.2). If you're interested, slide through all the options in the Settings menu. You'll find that you can set such things as the type of emulation, terminal preferences, the protocol used for binary transfers, and the modem command strings. Make any changes that are relevant. If you have a fairly standard setup then the defaults should work.

To connect to a machine, choose the **Dial** option in the Phone menu. You can enter a phone number in the text field, or you can set a default phone number in the **Phone Number** option of the Settings menu. If the **Dial** option is not available, it means that no COM port has been selected. Select one in the **Communications** option of the Settings menu. If the terminal successfully connects to the machine then you're ready to go. Press return once or twice, log it, then proceed. If you encounter problems, then it has fallen upon you to enter the pit of doom that defines modem communications. You basically have to become an expert to debug anything. The problem is probably in the communications parameters, so try changing them. It's best to find someone who knows what's going on if you're not an expert yourself.

The Transfers menu lets you initiate a transfer and send or receive a file. For example, on the system you've logged in to, you can ask it to initiate a file transfer using either Kermit or XModem. Once the transfer's initiated, you can choose the **Receive Binary file** options in the Transfers menu and receive the file (see instructions on the computer you are connected to for instructions on initiating transfers).

The Terminal application has several handy features you should know about. For example, you can echo the current session to the printer to keep a record of it. You can also use the timer mode to keep track of your connection time. To see the timer, however, you have to enable the function key display (its the last entry in the Settings menu). You can copy and paste things through the Clipboard or change the font to make the screen easier to read.

When you're finished, choose the **Hangup** option in the Phone menu and exit. If you changed anything in the Settings menu, a dialog appears asking if you want to save the new settings. Once they're saved, you can reload those settings the next time you want to use Terminal by double-clicking on the settings file, or changing the Terminal icon in the Program Manager.

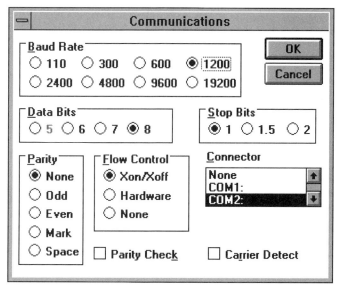

Figure 11.2
The Communications Settings dialog.

11.3 Common Questions

 How do I change the communications settings?
You can change the settings (baud rate, parity, etc.) with the **Communications** option in the Settings menu, or with the **Ports** applet in the Control Panel.

? *How do I change the modem commands for different modems?*
Use the **Modem Commands** option in the Settings menu.

? *How do I save my settings so I don't have to keep changing them every time I use Terminal?*
You can save the current settings using the **Save** option in the File menu. You can use the **Open** option in the File menu to reload settings, or double-click on a settings file in the File Manager.

? *How do I make the Terminal program automatically load a settings file every time I double-click on its icon?*
See the previous question to create a settings file. Then click on the **Terminal** icon in the Program Manager and select the **Properties** option in the File menu. Change the Command Line string to contain the settings file (include the path or change the Working Directory string to the path).

? *How do I make Terminal remember and use different settings? I have two modems on two different COM ports and they take different settings.*
Save two settings files and load each one depending on which modem you wish to use. Load the settings file with the **File | Open** command or by double-clicking on it in the File Manager.

? *How do I transfer a file from a remote system to my system?*
First, make sure you have adequate disk space available to receive the file. Terminal supports Kermit and XModem transfer protocols. Pick one and, on the remote system, type the command that initiates a transfer. See the documentation on that system for instructions. In Terminal choose the **Receive Binary File** option in the Transfers menu. The transfer will begin and complete automatically.

? *How do I stop a transfer after it has started?*
Click on the **Stop** button or choose **Stop** in the Transfers menu.

? *Why is the **Dial** option disabled?*
The COM port selection is invalid or you need to set the phone number. Set the COM port in the **Communications** option of the Settings menu.

 Is there a way to create a log file on the disk?
Create a generic printer in the Print Manager that causes the printout to
go to disk. Then send the print log to that printer using the **File | Print
Setup** option.

 I have enabled the timer mode but I don't see a timer anywhere. Where is it?
Select the **Show Function Keys** option in the Settings menu.

 *I dialed one number, but now I want to dial another. Every time I choose
Dial it dials the old number. How do I change the phone number?*
Use the **Phone Number** option in the Settings menu.

11.4 Details

11.4.1   The File Menu

The File menu lets you open and save settings files.

11.4.1.1   The File | New Option

This option lets you create a new set of settings. It returns all settings to
their default values. If the current settings have not been saved you'll be
prompted.

11.4.1.2   The File | Open Option

This option allows you to open a settings file previously saved to disk. It
is therefore possible to keep several different settings files on disk, one for each
of your common modem sessions.

11.4.1.3   The File | Save Option

This option saves the current settings to disk. The file can then be reload-
ed later using the **Open** option or by double-clicking on it in the File Manager.

11.4.1.4   The File | Save As Option

This option allows you to enter a new file name to save the current settings.

11.4.1.5   The File | Print Setup Option

This option lets you set up the printer for the **Settings | Printer Echo** option.

11.4.1.6   The File | Exit Option

The **Exit** option terminates the application. If the settings were changed you'll see a dialog asking if you wish to save the changes.

11.4.2   The Edit Menu

This menu allows you to use the Clipboard in the current session. The Clipboard can be extremely useful for saving pieces of the session or sending text from other applications to a remote system.

11.4.2.1   The Edit | Copy Option

This option copies the selected text onto the Clipboard. You can then paste it into Notepad, Write, or other applications that accept text.

11.4.2.2   The Edit | Paste Option

This option pastes the contents of the Clipboard into the Terminal window and sends it out over the modem as though you'd typed it on the keyboard.

11.4.2.3   The Edit | Send Option

This option copies the selection to the Clipboard and then immediately pastes it back into the window (to avoid having to cut and paste as separate actions).

11.4.2.4   The Edit | Select All Option

This option selects the entire buffer in the terminal window. You can set the buffer length in the **Terminal Preferences** dialog in the Settings menu.

11.4.2.5   The Edit | Clear Buffer Option

The terminal buffer lets you scroll through lines that have already left the screen. This option clears the entire buffer. You can set the buffer length in the Terminal Preferences dialog in the Settings menu.

11.4.3   The Settings Menu

This menu lets you determine all the different settings for the modem, terminal, and communications port. You can return to default settings by selecting the **New** option in the Settings menu.

11.4.3.1   The Settings | Phone Number Option

This option lets you set the phone number, whether or not it re-dials, and the timeout time for a connection (see Figure 11.3).

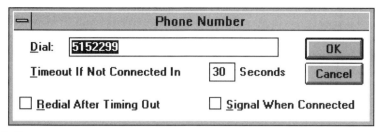

Figure 11.3
The Phone Number dialog.

11.4.3.2   The Settings | Terminal Emulation Option

This option allows you to choose between VT-100, VT-52, and TTY terminal emulators.

11.4.3.3   The Settings | Terminal Preferences Option

This option lets you set your terminal preferences. You can set the terminal mode, the number of columns, the font, the treatment of line feed characters, the cursor, and translations. You can also set the size of the terminal buffer you can scroll through (see Figure 11.4).

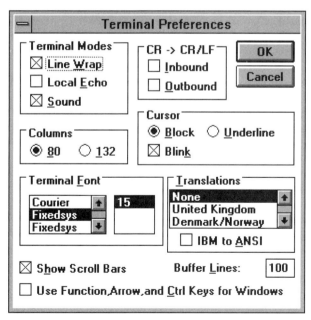

Figure 11.4
The Terminal Preferences Dialog.

11.4.3.4   The Settings I Function Keys Option

This option lets you assign strings to the different function keys. When you press the function key (or click on the function key buttons shown on screen) the string is copied into the terminal as though you had typed it (see Figure 11.5). In the figure, the Key Name field is a label that goes on a button displayed on the screen (see Section 11.4.3.11) while the command is the string generated by the function key.

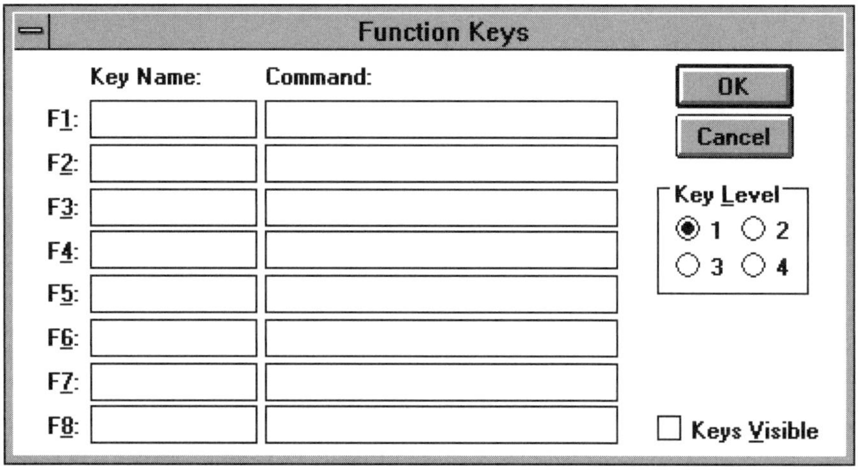

Figure 11.5

The Function Keys dialog.

11.4.3.5   The Settings I Text Transfers Option

Terminal can transfer text files using no error checking. This is risky but normally faster than Kermit because Kermit corrects any error by retransmitting blocks. This option lets you set the type of flow control, as shown in Figure 11.6. Generally, it's a better idea to use a binary transfer mode because it will correct errors.

11.4.3.6   The Settings I Binary Transfers Option

This option lets you choose the XModem or Kermit transfer protocols for binary transfers.

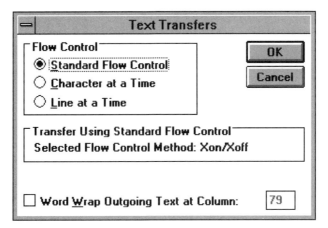

Figure 11.6
The Text Transfers dialog.

11.4.3.7   The Settings | Communications Option

This dialog lets you choose the communications parameters for the COM port. The **Ports** option in the Control Panel is another way to set these (see Figure 11.7).

11.4.3.8   The Settings | Modem Commands Option

This option lets you set the command strings for the modem (see Figure 11.8).

11.4.3.9   The Settings | Printer Echo Option

When this option is checked, all data that appears in the window is echoed to the default printer. Use the **Printer Setup** option in the File menu to set up the printer.

11.4.3.10   The Settings | Timer Mode Option

When this option is checked, the timer mode is enabled and phone calls will be timed. Choose the **Show Function Keys** option to display the timer.

11.4.3.11   The Settings | Function Keys Option

This option displays the function keys set with the dialog described in section 11.4.3.4.

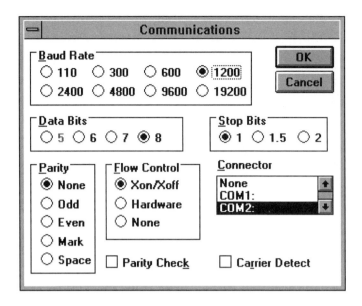

Figure 11.7
The Communications dialog.

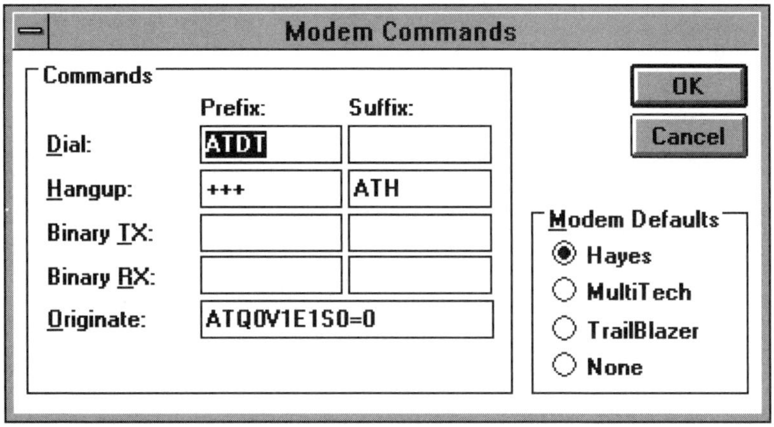

Figure 11.8
The Modem Commands dialog.

11.4.4   The Phone Menu

This menu lets you dial and hang up the phone.

11.4.4.1   The Phone | Dial Option

This option dials the last number or the number set using the **Phone Number** dialog in the Settings menu.

11.4.4.2   The Phone | Hangup Option

This option hangs up the modem.

11.4.5   The Transfers Menu

This menu lets you transfer files between machines.

11.4.5.1   The Transfers | Send Text File Option

This option begins a text file transfer immediately and sends the file down the wire. The other end will see the file coming as though the user were typing on the keyboard.

11.4.5.2   The Transfers | Receive Text File Option

This option causes the Terminal program to begin receiving a text file. Generally this is only useful when the remote system is another copy of Terminal. When the file is complete click on the **Stop** button.

11.4.5.3   The Transfers | View Text File Option

This option displays the selected text file in the Terminal window.

11.4.5.4   The Transfers | Send Binary File Option

This option begins a binary transfer using either the XModem or Kermit protocols. Use the **Settings | Binary Transfers** menu option to set the protocol. You must type a command on the machine you are connected to so it's ready to receive the file before choosing this option (see instructions on the remote system to learn how to do this).

11.4.5.5   The Transfers | Receive Binary File Option

This option causes Terminal to begin receiving a binary file. Use the **Settings | Binary Transfers** menu option to set the protocol. You must type a command on the machine you are connected to so it's ready to send the file before choosing this option (see instructions on the remote system to learn how to do this). Make sure you have adequate disk space before beginning the transfer.

11.4.5.6 The Transfers | Pause Option

This option pauses a file transfer.

11.4.5.7 The Transfers | Resume Option

This option resumes a file transfer after a pause.

11.4.5.8 The Transfers | Stop Option

This option stops a file transfer midstream.

S CHEDULE

12

Used properly, a computer can really help you to organize yourself. By putting your daily schedule on-line you let your computer keep track not only of daily appointments, but of events such as birthdays and anniversaries that will not happen for many months.

The Schedule+ application and the Mail program (see Chapter 17) work together very closely. If your machine is connected to a network and you expect to be using e-mail, you should read Chapter 17 first. If you are not connected to a network or e-mail system you will use Schedule+ in its stand-alone mode (referred to as "off-line"). In that case, you can start on this chapter now.

12.1 Executive Summary

The Schedule+ application is a daily appointment organizer and reminder system. It is also a "groupware" program. It helps groups of NT users connected by a network to stay organized. In conjunction with e-mail (see Chapter 17), this program allows people to organize and schedule meetings without playing phone tag. It also allows people to look at each other's schedules to pick meeting times that avoid conflicts.

Used by itself, Schedule+ is an extremely powerful program. A typical screen is shown in Figure 12.1. It lets you keep track of your daily schedule in the same way you would use a day-timer. Unlike a day-timer, however, you can set audible alarms that go off prior to the meeting. The calendar area lets you quickly look at another day's schedule by clicking on the day in question, and the notes area lets you enter reminder notes for each day. You can get a good idea of your free time during the week by using the Planner option. It shows the whole week at a glance with all meeting and appointment times blocked off (see Figure 12.2).

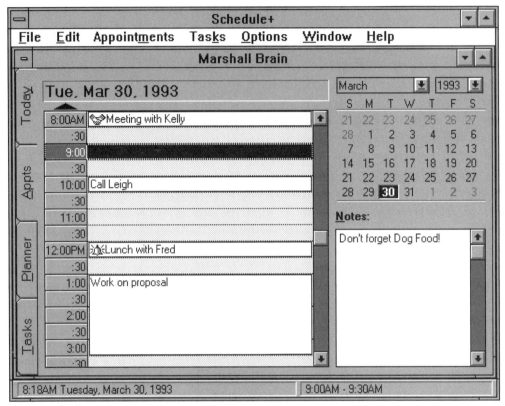

Figure 12.1
The Schedule+ application.

Schedule+ helps you prioritize your time by keeping track of projects and tasks. You can create a new project and subdivide it into individual tasks, or create independent tasks. You can then set reminders on your tasks and also block out time in your schedule to accomplish your projects.

When you schedule a meeting, you can automatically send e-mail to everyone who should attend. They can respond by accepting or rejecting your invitation. When people accept, they are automatically added to the list of attendees for the meeting. You will also receive meeting invitations from other people. You can respond by accepting, tentatively accepting, or declining.

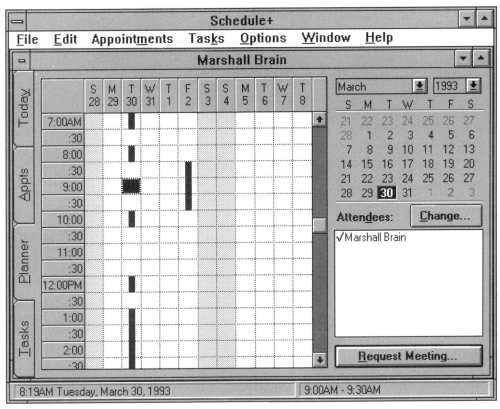

Figure 12.2
The Schedule+ Planner.

Schedule+ is useful for scheduling resources such as conference rooms. Simply create a mailbox for the resource and people will be able to view its schedule and allocate its time.

12.2 Guided Tour

Schedule+ works very closely with the e-mail system to take advantage of its groupware features. If you're not connected to a Post Office and don't plan to be, you can use the scheduler in its "off-line" mode. It will save information in a file on your local hard disk. If you plan to use e-mail, however, and want to take advantage of the groupware features of Schedule+, then you should connect to an e-mail Post Office before using Schedule+ (see Chapter 17 for details). Connecting to a Post Office after you've used Schedule+ in its stand-alone mode is difficult.

To start the Schedule+ application, double-click on its icon in the Main group of the Program Manager. If you are not connected to a Post Office, then the first time you start up the scheduler you'll see a dialog asking if you want to work off-line. If you do not, go to Chapter 17 and get connected. If you do, answer affirmatively. You will be asked to create an account name and password (the default password is "PASSWORD") and then to specify a message file on your local disk. Once everything's set up you're ready to start using the scheduler. If you are already connected to a Post Office you'll probably be asked to log in to the mail system. Once you're logged in you can begin working.

When the program begins execution it displays today's appointments in the Appointment mode (see Figure 12.1). There are two ways to create an appointment:

1. Single-click on a line in your schedule and enter a description of the activity set for that time. You can also drag over several lines to create a block of time longer than half an hour and then type into that block of time. This technique is good for making quick, simple entries.

2. Select the **New Appointment** option in the Appointment menu or double-click on a line in your schedule. A dialog appears that lets you select the exact starting and ending time for the meeting. You can also enter a description here and set a reminder that will go off at a specified time before the activity's scheduled time. If you mark the appointment as **Private,** then other people viewing your appointment book will not be able to read the description. You can also click on the **Invite** button to invite people to a meeting. Click on the names of those people you wish to invite and add them to the list. When you click the OK button of the New Appointment dialog, you can send e-mail to each person you've invited.

It is also possible to create recurring appointments by selecting the **New Recurring Appointments** option in the Appointments menu. You can specify not only the time but the frequency of the meetings so your schedule always contains that appointment at each interval.

You can easily delete, copy, edit, and move appointments using the corresponding menu options in the Edit menu. The Appointment menu also allows you to mark appointments as tentative or private. The alarm feature can be toggled on and off using the **Set Reminder** toggle.

Once you've created several appointments, flip to the Planner mode by clicking on the **Planner** tab along the left side of the window. In this mode you can see your week at a glance with the scheduled times blocked out. There are several interesting features in the Planner mode. First, you can drag over a block of time and then select the **New Appointment** option to describe the appointment at that time. You can also overlay other people's schedules on top of your own by clicking on the **Change** button above the attendees list. The schedules of all selected attendees will appear and you can easily see non-conflicting times. You can select a time by clicking on it or dragging over several blocks, or you can choose the **Auto-Pick** option in the Appointments menu. It will pick the next free meeting time for you. Before choosing **Auto-Pick** you should drag over the amount of time the meeting will occupy.

It's possible to view and even change other people's appointment books if they've given you permission to do so. In the same way, it's possible to give an assistant the ability to view and change your appointment book. The **Set Access Privileges** option in the Options menu lets you select who can see and modify your schedule. The system will default to View mode for everyone. This permission gives you the right to overlay other people's blocked out time on your planner. If you like you can give everyone the right to read your schedule and create or modify appointments, or you can just give it to specific individuals. You can designate assistants to manipulate your schedule in the same way you can. You can also shut off your schedule so no one can view it in any way by choosing the None privilege. Whatever privileges you give to the default group apply to everyone who can access your schedule.

Use the **Open Other's Appt. Book** option in the File menu to view someone else's appointment book. If they've given you permission you'll see their appointment book and read all appointments that are not private.

Select the **General Options** option in the Option menu. Here you can specify several default behaviors for the system. For example, you can indicate whether reminders (alarms) are set automatically, and how long before the appointment the alarm goes off. You can also specify when your day typically starts and ends so others planning meetings around your schedule know your normal hours.

The other important facility in Schedule+ is the Task handler. For example, the system can help you to remember tasks, such as your weekly report to the budget committee, or projects such as your new class outlines. It will let you budget time to accomplish your tasks and remind you as their due dates approach. Click on the **Tasks** tab to the left of the window and a blank list appears. Add a task by selecting the **New Task** option in the Tasks menu. Alternately, you can create a new project and divide it into separate tasks by adding them to the project. When you create a task you can specify its due date and its starting time. You can also indicate priority.

By selecting a task in the list you can mark it as completed, or you can add time for it to your schedule. Click on the appropriate button at the bottom of the window. The Tasks menu lets you sort and view the tasks in several different ways, and also allows you to create recurring tasks in the same way used for recurring appointments.

12.3 Common Questions

? *How do I make the Schedule+ application automatically start up whenever I log in?*

Copy the Schedule+ icon, in the Main group of the Program Manager, into the Start-up Group (see Chapter 2). If you want the icon to automatically log you in as well, select the icon, choose the **Properties** option in the **File** menu, and add your user name and password to the command line (e.g., "SCHEDPL32.EXE brain passwd"). Don't use this feature unless you're certain your account and its file system are secure. If they're not secure, others could potentially discover your e-mail password. This auto log in feature will not work with a null password.

? *How do I set an alarm for 3:42 PM next Wednesday?*

Choose the **New Appointments** option in the Appointments menu. In the dialog, select 3:42 PM on Wednesday as the starting time and the ending time as appropriate. Set a reminder for the time and have the reminder go off zero minutes beforehand. At the appointed time the system will beep.

? *What happens if I am not logged in or the Schedule+ program is not running when an alarm goes off?*

Nothing. The alarm is ignored. It's up to you to review your schedule and see what you missed.

Each day starts at 8:00 AM when I look at the daily screens, but I normally come into work at 6:00 AM. How do I make each day start earlier?
Use the **Options | General Options** option to set starting and ending times for your typical day.

How do I print a paper copy to carry with me on trips?
Use the **File | Print** option and print out the days you want to take with you.

How do I manage a resource like a conference room?
Your e-mail administrator can create an e-mail account for the resource, just like it was another person. This e-mail account should be marked as a resource in the General Options dialog (see Figure 12.3). You can then set yourself up as an assistant to this account and manage the room's scheduling, or allow anyone to edit the room's appointment book to schedule a time.

There are a hundred people on our e-mail system, so it takes a long time to pick attendees for a meeting. How do I reduce the list to the ones I'm interested in?
The Rolodex icon lets you enter specific people into a personal Rolodex. You can then view that list when picking people to invite to a meeting (see Chapter 17 for details on the personal Rolodex).

I have been using the scheduler in stand-alone mode but now I want to connect to a Post Office to interact with a group. How do I tell the program to connect?
First you should use the **Export** option in the File menu to save your current schedule. Export it in Schedule+ format and save the resulting file someplace safe. Now try to go on-line with the **File | Online** option. You will probably get an error message having to do with MSMAIL.INI. This file controls your connection to the e-mail server. You can do one of two things: Either erase this file completely and then run the Mail application (it will think it's being initialized for the first time and ask for the name of the Post Office), or open the file with Notepad (see Chapter 8)

and change the **ServerPath** line to point to the location of the Post
Office on the network. A typical network location will have the format
\\computername\dirname.... Your administrator may have to help with
this if the file system is secure.

12.4 Details

12.4.1   The File Menu

This menu lets you manipulate and print calendar files.

12.4.1.1   The File | Turn Off/On Reminders Option

This option turns off the ability of Schedule+ to remind you of an appointment.

12.4.1.2   The File | Work Offline/Online Option

When you choose the **Offline** option, Schedule+ copies all the information it needs from the e-mail system to a local file and disconnects from e-mail.
This is especially handy if you have a portable computer that you are discon-
necting from the network to take with you. When you return on-line, all
changes are copied to the e-mail server as needed.

12.4.1.3   The File | Move Local File Option

This option lets you change the directory in which your local copy of the
schedule is stored.

12.4.1.4   The File | Open Other's Appt. Book Option

This option allows you to open another user's appointment book. The
option is only valid if the user in question has given you Read, Add, or Change
permission concerning their appointments (since you'll see any appointments
not marked Private). If the other user has given you only View permissions,
then use the Planner mode and change the attendees list.

12.4.1.5   The File | Export Appointments Option

This option allows you to export your appointments either in Schedule+
format or text format. You can then import them elsewhere.

12.4.1.6 The File | Import Appointments Option

This option lets you import scheduling information that was exported using the previous option.

12.4.1.7 The File | Create Archive Option

The **Create Archive** option lets you archive historical data that is no longer useful. You will be asked to select the ending date for the archive, and all data between the system starting date and the archive date will be saved to the file name selected in the dialog that follows.

12.4.1.8 The File | Open Archive Option

This option lets you load and review archival data. Select the file that you wish to load.

12.4.1.9 The File | Print Option

This option lets you print out scheduling information. You can select the time frame and choose whether you want the information printed by day, week, or month. You can also print your task list.

12.4.1.10 The File | Print Setup Option

This option lets you pick and set the default printer and the margins.

12.4.1.11 The File | Exit Option

This option exits Schedule+ but leaves the reminder system running so you're reminded of meetings.

12.4.1.12 The File | Exit and Sign Out Option

This option exits Schedule+ and terminates the reminder system so you're not advised of upcoming meetings and appointments.

12.4.2 The Edit Menu

This menu lets you edit appointments and tasks, and also work with the Clipboard.

12.4.2.1 The Edit | Undo Option

This option undoes the previous action.

12.4.2.2   The Edit | Cut Option

This option cuts the selected text onto the Clipboard.

12.4.2.3   The Edit | Copy Option

This option copies the selected text onto the Clipboard.

12.4.2.4   The Edit | Paste Option

This option pastes the contents of the Clipboard into the current time slot.

12.4.2.5   The Edit | Edit Appt/Task Option

This option lets you edit an existing appointment or task. An alternate method is to double-click on the appointment or task.

12.4.2.6   The Edit | Copy Appt Option

This option lets you copy an existing appointment to the Clipboard.

12.4.2.7   The Edit | Move Appt... Option

This option lets you move an existing appointment to a new time slot.

12.4.2.8   The Edit | Delete Appt/Task Option

This option deletes the selected appointment or task.

12.4.2.9   The Edit | Find Option

This option lets you search through all your appointment descriptions for a key word. You can search forward or backward from the current day, or you can search the entire file.

12.4.2.10   The Edit | Go To Date... Option

This option takes you to a specific day in the system. An alternative is to click on the day in the month calendar.

12.4.3   The Appointments Menu

This menu lets you create and adjust appointments.

12.4.3.1   The Appointments | New Appointment Option

This option lets you create a new appointment. An alternative is to double-click on a time slot.

12.4.3.2   The Appointments | Auto-Pick Option

In Planner mode, this option picks the next meeting time open to the listed attendees, starting at the currently selected time. When you add attendees to the Attendees list, their schedules are overlaid on top of yours and Auto-Pick will choose the next free slot.

12.4.3.3   The Appointments | New Recurring Appt Option

This option lets you create a new recurring appointment (e.g., a weekly meeting or a monthly event). You can specify the period of recurrence by clicking on the **Change** button in the dialog.

12.4.3.4   The Appointments | Edit Recurring Appts Option

This option lets you modify an existing recurring appointment. Choose the recurring appointment from the list. Alternately, you can double-click on the item in the list.

12.4.3.5   The Appointments | Tentative Option

This option lets you mark an appointment as tentative.

12.4.3.6   The Appointments | Private Option

This option lets you mark an appointment as private. No one viewing your appointment book is able to read the description of a private entry, but they can see that the time is blocked off.

12.4.3.7   The Appointments | Set Reminder Option

This option lets you set and remove the reminder (represented by an alarm bell) from an appointment. Appointments automatically pick up the reminder unless you specify otherwise in General Options.

12.4.3.8   The Appointments | Re-Send Mail Option

This option retransmits e-mail to the attendees of the selected meeting.

12.4.4   The Tasks Menu

This menu lets you add and edit tasks and projects.

168 Sec. 12.4 Details

12.4.4.1   The Tasks | New Task Option

This option lets you create a new task for yourself. In the dialog you name the task, choose a project for it if desired (you can also have tasks independent of any project), assign a due date and starting date and set the priority. By clicking on the **Tasks** tab you can allocate time for the given task in your schedule.

12.4.4.2   The Tasks | New Project Option

This option lets you name a new project. A project consists of just a name. You create tasks under the project name to help organize related tasks.

12.4.4.3   The Tasks | New Recurring Task Option

This option lets you create a recurring task in the same way that you create a recurring appointment. You can specify the period of the task, its start time and its due date.

12.4.4.4   The Tasks | Edit Recurring Tasks Option

This option allows you to edit a recurring task and change its frequency.

12.4.4.5   The Tasks | View by Project Option

This option lets you sort your task list by projects.

12.4.4.6   The Tasks | Sort by Priority Option

This option sorts your task list by the priority of your tasks.

12.4.4.7   The Tasks | Sort by Due Date Option

This option sorts your task list by the due dates of your tasks.

12.4.4.8   The Tasks | Sort by Description Option

This option sorts tasks alphabetically by description.

12.4.4.9   The Tasks | Show Active Tasks Option

This option causes the task list to display only those tasks that have actually started (according to their start dates).

12.4.5   The Options Menu

This menu lets you adjust the behavior of the scheduler.

12.4.5.1 The Options | Change Password Option

This option lets you change your password. This password applies both to your e-mail account and your schedule files.

12.4.5.2 The Options | Set Access Privileges Option

This option lets you determine how other users will be able to view your appointment book. You can lock them out completely, let them view only your times (your times are overlaid on theirs in the Planner mode), read your non-private appointments, add appointments, or change appointments. You can also assign an assistant with permission to do anything with your appointment book.

12.4.5.3 The Options | Display Option

This option lets you adjust the colors used to display your appointment book.

12.4.5.4 The Options | General Options Option

This option lets you set the default behavior of reminders as well as the starting and ending time for your typical day. You can also specify that an account be specifically used for allocating a resource such as a conference room (see Figure 12.3).

12.4.5.5 The Options | Status Bar Option

This option turns the Status bar on and off.

General Options

☐ Startup Offline

┌─Reminders────────────────────────────────────┐
│ ☒ Set Reminders for Notes   │
│ ☒ Set Reminders Automatically   │
│   for [15] [minute(s) ▼] before appointments │
│ ☒ Sound Audible Alarm   │
└───┘

Day Starts at: [7:00AM ▲▼]

Day Ends at: [7:00PM ▲▼]

Week Starts on: [Sunday   ▼]

☐ Show Week Numbers in the Calendar

☐ Send Meeting Messages Only to my Assistant

☐ This Account is for a Resource

[OK]   [Cancel]

Figure 12.3
The General Options dialog.

CARDFILE

13

Most people build data structures the old-fashioned way, on scraps of paper. For example, in my pocket right now I have a note about the dry cleaners, a piece of paper with a phone number, a list of expenses for today, and hand-written directions to my hotel. People also keep more organized data collections like address lists and recipe files, usually on index cards.

By simulating a box of index cards, the Cardfile application lets you duplicate these simple data structures in Windows NT. In this chapter we discuss how to use Cardfile to organize bits of information.

13.1 Executive Summary

The Cardfile application is like a deck of index cards. Each card can hold text or a picture. Like real index cards, the cards in Cardfile have a finite size. And although they can contain almost anything, there is no preset format and no way to divide the card into fields. Each card contains a text index line along the top that's used to sort the cards and display them as a deck.

Figure 13.1 shows a screen dump of the Cardfile application. Cards can also hold bitmaps. Because the Cardfile application has this ability to hold pictures in a compact format, it's useful for creating a scrapbook of images. It's especially useful for linking to a group of bitmap images stored on disk so you can preview the images easily.

Cardfile is an OLE client application (see the Guided Tour in Chapter 10 for a description of the different OLE modes).

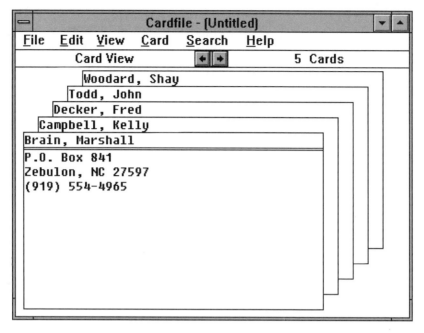

Figure 13.1
A typical card file.

13.2 Guided Tour

Start the Cardfile application by double-clicking on the **Cardfile** icon in
the Accessories group of the Program Manager. The program will initially display a single blank card. As a demonstration of the capabilities of this application, we'll create a simple address list.

Double-click on the top line of the card (or choose the **Index** option in
the Edit menu). This is the *index line.* The cards in the deck are sorted by the
index lines. In the dialog box that appears type your name, last name first. In
the body of the card, type your address.

Now add a new card by selecting the **Add** option in the Card menu and
entering another name and address. Add three or four cards this way. Notice
that you can click on the index line of any card to bring it to the front of the
deck.

In the View menu you can change the view of the deck from card view to
list view. In list view only the index lines are shown. If you double-click on any
index line you can change it.

Once you've created several cards you can try out the Search menu. The **Go To** option searches the index lines and the **Find** option searches the body of the card. Both options are case-insensitive and helpfully find partial matches (e.g., the word "John" matches both "john" and "johnson").

It's also possible to paste images from the Paintbrush application onto a card. To do so, add a new card to the deck and set its index line. Then, in the Edit menu, choose the **Picture** option. Now, get an image onto the Clipboard by opening a Paintbrush file and copying part or all of it (see Chapter 9 for a description of Paintbrush). Since Cardfile is an OLE client application, you can either paste, link, or embed the image on the card. The newly pasted image will shrink to fit the card when it's displayed on screen. If you double-click on the image it appears full-size in the Paintbrush program. This feature makes Cardfile useful as a scrapbook of images. It becomes a sort of multiple-entry Clipboard.

You can print individual cards or the entire deck using the **Print** options in the File menu.

13.3 Common Questions

I want to create a scrapbook of images. How can I do that?
Use the Cardfile application and paste each image onto a different card.

How do I create an address list? What is the best application to use?
Use the Cardfile application and place a different address on each card. Alternatively you can type the list into an editor such as Notepad or Write.

How can I make the Cardfile application load a certain file automatically when I double-click on its icon?
Click on the icon and choose the **File | Properties** option. In the **Command Line** field include the name of the card file as a parameter. You can include the path to the file on the command line, or place it in the **Working Directory** field.

How can I make the Cardfile application automatically start each time I log in?
Copy the Cardfile icon into the Start-up group (see Chapter 2).

I copied a Paintbrush image onto the Clipboard and I know it's there, but the Paste options are not available in Cardfile. Why not?
The current card is in Text mode. Use the **Picture** option in the Edit menu to change it to Picture mode.

13.4 Details

13.4.1   The File Menu

This menu lets you load and save Cardfile files, as well as print the contents of a file.

13.4.1.1   The File | New Option

This option lets you create a new card file. If the current file contains changes you'll be prompted to save the changes before a new file is created.

13.4.1.2   The File | Open Option

This option allows you to open an existing file stored on disk.

13.4.1.3   The File | Save Option

This option saves the current card file to disk so you can reload it later. If the file has not been saved before you'll be prompted for a new file name.

13.4.1.4   The File | Save As Option

The **Save As** option lets you save the current file to a new file name. Type the new name into the edit area.

13.4.1.5   The File | Print Option

This option prints the cards in the deck to the default printer. Use the **Page Setup** option to set headers, footers, and margins. Use the **Print Setup** option to customize the printer.

13.4.1.6   The File | Print All Option

This option prints the entire deck of cards to the default printer.

13.4.1.7   The File | Page Setup Option

This option lets you set margins and set the header and footer text. The following special characters, embedded in the header or footer string, can be used:

&d	The current date
&p	Page Numbers
&f	The file name
&l	All text following the &l code is aligned flush left
&c	All text following the &c code is centered
&r	All text following the &r code is aligned flush right
&t	The time at the start of the print job

13.4.1.8   The File | Print Setup Option

This option lets you choose the printer and its settings.

13.4.1.9   The File | Merge Option

This option lets you merge two card files together. When you choose the option you'll see an Open dialog that requests a new file name. The file will be opened and inserted into the current deck.

13.4.1.10   The File | Exit Option

This option terminates the Cardfile program. If the current deck has not been saved you will be prompted to save it.

13.4.2   The Edit Menu

This menu gives you access to the Clipboard. Cardfile is an OLE client, so it can embed or link from other OLE servers such as the Paintbrush application.

13.4.2.1   The Edit | Undo Option

This option undoes the previous action.

13.4.2.2   The Edit | Cut Option

This option cuts the currently selected text or graphic onto the Clipboard so it can be pasted elsewhere.

13.4.2.3   The Edit | Copy Option

This option copies the currently selected text or graphic onto the Clipboard so it can be pasted elsewhere.

13.4.2.4   The Edit | Paste Option

This option pastes the contents of the Clipboard onto the current card. If the Clipboard entry was placed there by an OLE server, then the object will be embedded (and can be edited by double-clicking on it). If not, it will simply be pasted.

13.4.2.5   The Edit | Paste Link Option

This option is only available if the current selection on the Clipboard was placed there by an OLE server such as Paintbrush (see Chapter 9). The Clipboard selection is linked. See the Guided Tour in Section 10.2 for a description of the differences between linking and embedding and an example.

If the **Paste Link** option is not available, it generally means that the file has not yet been saved in the OLE server. Save the file in the server and recopy the selection to the Clipboard.

13.4.2.6   The Edit | Paste Special Option

This option is only available if the current selection on the Clipboard was placed there by an OLE server such as Paintbrush (see Chapter 9). You'll see the dialog shown in Figure 10.3 when you select the option. This dialog shows you the source, the different formats in which the data was placed on the Clipboard, and several buttons. Use the default format. If you click the **Paste** button the selection is embedded (equivalent to the **Paste** option in the **Edit** menu). If you click on the **Paste Link** button the selection is linked (equivalent to the **Paste Link** option in the **Edit** menu). See the Guided Tour in section 10.2 for a description of the differences and an example.

If the **Paste Link** button is not available, it generally means the file has not yet been saved in the OLE server. Save the file in the server and recopy the selection to the Clipboard.

13.4.2.7   The Edit | Index Option

This option lets you edit the index line of the current card. Alternately, you can double-click on the index line to edit it.

13.4.2.8   The Edit | Restore Option

This option is like undo. It restores a card to its previous contents.

13.4.2.9   The Edit | Text Option

This option sets the current card to text mode.

13.4.2.10   The Edit | Picture Option

This option sets the current card to picture mode. This mode must be set in order to paste a graphic image onto the card.

13.4.2.11   The Edit | Link Option

This option displays a dialog that lets you view the link information about a linked object on the current card. You can specify whether links are automatically or manually updated in this dialog.

13.4.2.12   The Edit | Edit...Object Option

This option lets you edit a linked or embedded object in the application from which it came. If the object is embedded you will see the object itself in its application. If it is linked, the application will bring up the file from which it is linked. An alternate method is to double-click on the object.

13.4.2.13   The Edit | Insert Object Option

This option allows you to embed a new object of the specified type. The appropriate application will execute and you can create the new object in it. When you click the **File | Update** option in the application and exit, the new object will appear in the current card.

13.4.3   The View Menu

This menu lets you switch between card and list modes.

13.4.3.1   The View | Card Option

The card mode displays the cards in a view that looks like a deck of cards. You can select and view any card by clicking on its index line.

13.4.3.2   The View | List Option

The list mode displays the cards in a view that shows all the index lines. This view allows more index lines to appear on the screen at one time.

13.4.4   The Card Menu

This menu lets you add and delete cards.

13.4.4.1   The Card | Add Option

This option adds a new card to the deck. You will be prompted to enter the index line for the new card.

13.4.4.2   The Card | Delete Option

This option deletes the current card.

13.4.4.3   The Card | Duplicate Option

This option duplicates the current card, including its index line. Double-click on the index line if you want to change it.

13.4.4.4   The Card | AutoDial Option

If you select a phone number on the current card, this option will dial it for you on your modem. If nothing is selected then autodial will pick the first number it finds. Use the **Setup** option to make the program conform to your modem.

13.4.5   The Search Menu

This menu allows you to quickly find a card in the deck.

13.4.5.1   The Search | Go To Option

This option accepts a string that is used to search index lines. The first matching card is displayed.

13.4.5.2   The Search | Find Option

This option accepts a string that is used to search the body of text cards. The first matching card is displayed. You can make the search case-sensitive or insensitive, and searching can proceed forward or backward through the deck.

13.4.5.3   The Search | Find Next Option

This option repeats the last Find operation starting at the current card.

Cᴌᴏᴄᴋ

14

No GUI is complete without a clock. Windows NT provides a simple clock that displays the time in both analog and digital modes.

14.1 Executive Summary

The Clock application displays the time in analog or digital format. You can re-size the clock to make it easy to read. The face will enlarge itself to fill as much of the available space as possible. You can also create an ultra-small display by minimizing the clock and it will continue to display the time on its icon. Figures 14.1 and 14.2 show the clock's analog and digital faces.

Figure 14.1
The analog clock.

Figure 14.2
The digital clock.

In digital mode the clock can display the date as well as the time. To make its display less insistent, you can also turn the second hand on and off.

14.2 Guided Tour

Start the Clock application by finding and double-clicking its icon in the Accessories group of the Program Manager. Look in the **Settings** menu for the **Analog** and **Digital** options to change between its analog and digital modes. Try minimizing it. The icon will continue to show the time in the chosen format. Restore the icon. Flip to digital mode and enable and disable the date display using the **Date** option (you cannot display the date in analog mode). You can also change the font while in digital mode using the **Font** option. Turn the second hand on and off as well.

There are many cases where you would like the clock to be visible at all times. You don't want it getting covered up by other windows, for example, when an important meeting is coming up. A special option in the System Menu called **Always On Top** (the small square at the left side of the Title Bar), causes the clock to float above the other windows on the desktop at all times.

You can minimize the space needed by the clock, and also make it look more symmetrical, by turning off the Title Bar. Use the **No Title** option to do this. To replace the Title Bar, double-click on the clock's face. To move the clock while the Title Bar is invisible, drag the face of the clock to a new position.

14.3 Common Questions

How do I set an alarm?
Use the Schedule+ program to set alarms (see Chapter 12).

The clock is always getting buried under other windows. How do I keep it visible all of the time?
Use the **Always On Top** option in the System Menu.

14.4 Details

The clock application is so simple that it needs only one menu: the Settings menu. Use it to control the clock's appearance.

14.4.1   The Settings I Analog Option

This option changes the clock to analog mode. Even if the Date option is selected it will not be displayed in this mode.

14.4.2   The Settings | Digital Option

This option changes the clock to digital mode.

14.4.3   The Settings | Set Font Option

This option lets you set the font used while in digital mode.

14.4.4   The Settings | No Title Option

When enabled this option removes the Title Bar. Double-click on the clock to replace the Title Bar.

14.4.5   The Settings | Seconds Option

This option enables and disables the seconds display.

14.4.6   The Settings | Date Option

This option enables and disables the date display while in digital mode.

14.4.7   The System | Always On Top Option

The System menu (click the small square on the left side of the title bar, or press Alt-space) contains the **Always On Top** option. Use it to force the clock to float above all other windows on the desktop at all times.

CALCULATOR

The Calculator application does just what you'd expect: it lets you put a calculator on the NT desktop. This chapter discusses the calculator and shows some of its advanced features.

15.1 Executive Summary

The Calculator application implements a desktop calculator that works the same as any pocket calculator. The application actually contains two calculators: a normal one and a scientific version. These two versions are shown in Figures 15.1 and 15.2.

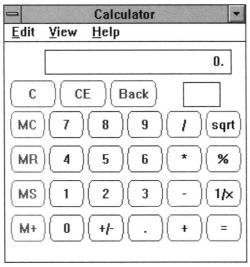

Figure 15.1
The standard calculator.

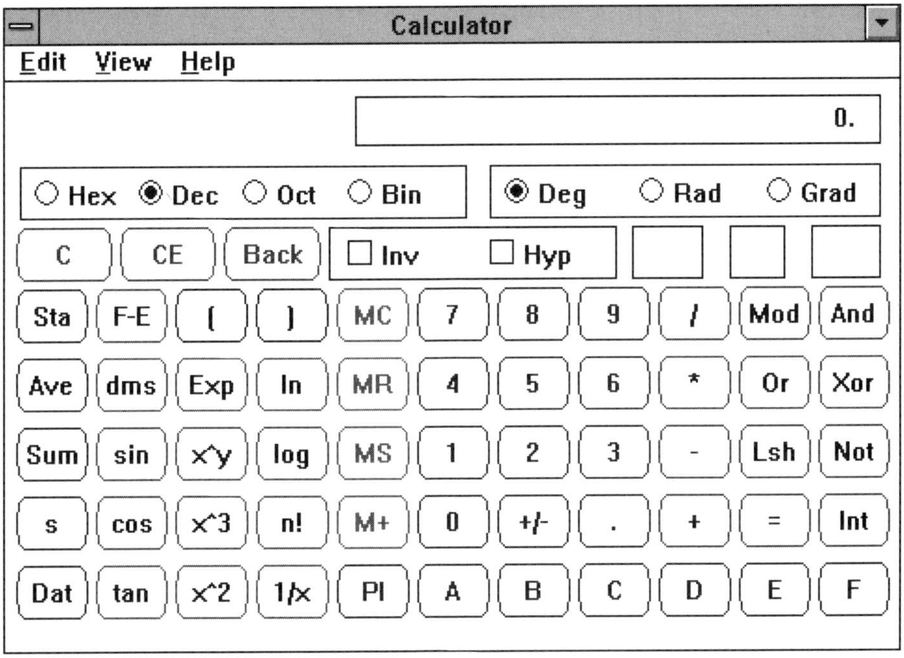

Figure 15.2
The scientific calculator.

The standard calculator contains the normal four functions, along with several extra keys for percentages, square roots, and reciprocals. It also has memory. The scientific calculator not only contains advanced scientific features such as Sin and Cos, exponents, logs, and statistical functions, but it also handles binary number conversions and functions that are extremely useful for programmers. You can convert between binary, octal, decimal, and hex number systems. You can also perform And, Or, Xor, and Not operations.

15.2 Guided Tour

Start the Calculator by double-clicking on its icon in the Accessories group of the Program Manager. A standard 12-digit pocket calculator appears on screen. This calculator works just like any normal pocket calculator, so most things should be intuitive. Click on the buttons with the mouse, or use the keyboard. Obvious keyboard mappings are used for the numbers and normal keys. For less obvious keys like Sqrt, see Section 15.4 for a complete listing of keyboard accelerators. Sqrt happens to use the "@" character in standard mode ("i@" in scientific mode). This calculator also understands the Clipboard. You can copy the current number to the Clipboard and paste it into other documents, or you can paste from the Clipboard to the calculator's display.

You enable the scientific calculator by choosing the **Scientific** option in the View menu. This calculator has standard scientific functions, statistical features, and a set of operations and conversions useful to programmers.

To use the statistical portion of the calculator, press the **Sta** button. A small modeless dialog appears. Because it's modeless you can use it simultaneously with the calculator; move it to one side to see both. Enter a number into the calculator and press the **Dat** button. Enter a second number and press **Dat** again. The dialog holds a list of all values entered. You can delete an invalid entry by clicking on it in the dialog and pressing the **CD** button, or clear all entries by pressing the **CAD** button. The **Load** button transfers the current selection to the display, and **Ret** returns focus to the calculator. Enter four or five numbers and press **Sum**. The number displayed is the sum of all data points in the dialog. Press **Ave** to get their average and **S** to find the standard deviation.

The programmer portion of the calculator lets you convert between binary, octal, decimal, and hex number systems. The A-F keys at the bottom of the display let you enter hex values when in hex mode. Try entering a number like 55, then convert it to the different number systems by clicking on each type. Binary operators on the right side of the calculator can also be used at any time, in any display format, in the same way the plus or minus keys might be used.

15.3 Common Questions

Where is the scientific calculator?
Choose the **Scientific** option in the View menu.

How do I use the statistics keys?
Press the **Sta** button to enable the statistical keys.

What do the A, B, C, D, E, and F keys do?
They are used to enter hexadecimal values.

How do I change to and from the exponential display?
Use the **F-E** button

How do I save myself from retyping the number from the calculator into my document?

Use the Edit menu to copy the value to the Clipboard and then paste it into your document.

15.4 Details

The following table shows the meaning of each button and its keyboard accelerator:

Operation	Keystroke	Description
+	+	Add
-	-	Subtract
*	*	Multiply
/	/	Divide
=	=	Calculate the answer
%	%	Percent
Sqrt	@	Square root
1/x	r	Reciprocal
+/-	F9	Flip the sign
.	.or,	Decimal point
Back	Backspace or Left Arrow	Deletes last digit
CE	Del	Clear the display
C	Esc	Clear last calculation
MC	Ctrl-L	Clears memory
MR	Ctrl-R	Recalls memory
MS	Ctrl-M	Stores the current value in memory
M+	Ctrl-P	Adds the current value to memory
(	(	
)	)	
And	&	Boolean And
Int	;	Strip fractional part of decimal number
Lsh	<	Boolean left shift

Operation	Keystroke	Description
Mod	%	Mod (remainder)
Not	~	Boolean Not
Or	|	Boolean Or
Xor	^	Boolean Xor
Bin	F8	Binary mode
Oct	F7	Octal mode
Dec	F6	Decimal mode
Hex	F5	Hex mode
Byte	F4	Byte size
Word	F3	Word size (16 bit)
DWord	F2	Double-word size (32 bit)
Sta	Ctrl-S	Enable stat mode
Dat	Ins	Enter data value
Sum	Ctrl-T	Sum
Ave	Ctrl-A	Average
s	Ctrl-D	Standard deviation
RET	Alt-R	Return focus to the calculator
LOAD	Alt-L	Copy the selected value to the display
CD	Alt-C	Clear the selected value
CAD	Alt-A	Clear all values
cos	o	Cosine
Deg	F2	Degrees
dms	m	Degree-minute-second format in display
Exp	x	Enter exponent for scientific notation
F-E	v	Flip between normal and scientific notation
Grad	F4	Gradients
Hyp	h	Hyperbolic Sin, Cos, and Tan

Operation	Keystroke	Description
Inv	i	Inverts Sin, Cos, Tan, PI, x^y, x^2, x^3, ln, log, Ave, Sum, s.
ln	n	Natural log
log	l	Base 10 log
n!	!	Factorial
PI	p	PI
Rad	F3	Radians
sin	s	Sine
tan	t	Tangent
x^y	y	X raised to the Y power
x^2	@	X squared
x^3	#	X cubed

CHARACTER MAP

There you are, typing along, when suddenly you need a special character. Trouble is, you have no idea where to find one. You might need a copyright symbol "," for example, or a trademark symbol "'," or something special like a Greek letter for an equation. What you need is the Character Map.

16.1 Executive Summary

Figure 16.1 shows a typical view of the Character Map application. It displays all the characters in a chosen font so you can copy them to the Clipboard and paste them elsewhere. This feature makes it extremely easy to find unusual characters and then insert them into your document.

16.2 Guided Tour

Start the Character Map application by double-clicking on its icon in the Accessories group of the Program Manager. You'll see all the characters in a particular font. Use the Font combo box in the upper left corner to choose a different font (two of the more interesting fonts are Symbols and Wingdings). The Symbols font, for example, contains the copyright symbol, the trademark symbol, the complete Greek alphabet in upper and lower case, and a wide variety of mathematical operators.

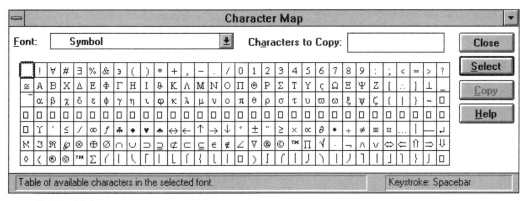

Figure 16.1
The Character Map application.

If you click on a character, you'll see an enlarged version that's easy to identify. For example, in the bottom right corner of the Wingdings font is a character that makes no sense until it's inflated. Clicking on it provides a better view and also highlights it. If you press the **Select** button, the character is displayed in the **Characters to Copy** field in the upper right corner of the window. Then, if you click on the **Copy** button, the character is copied to the Clipboard where it can be pasted into any document.

It's also possible to type characters directly into a document without going through the Clipboard. You simply enter the characters from the keyboard as though you were typing normal characters. To do this, you need to know which key on the keyboard generates the desired character. One way to figure this out is to display the Symbol font in the Character Map window and note the position of the character you want. Then choose a "normal" font like Times or Arial and display it in the window. Note the character at the same position. When you type that character while the word processor is in the Symbol font, the desired character is generated. As an example, say you want to create a capital Sigma in a document. Display the Symbol font in the Character Map window, find the Sigma, then display the Times font. The normal capital "S" character occupies the same location, so typing a capital S while in the Symbol font will create a capital Sigma.

16.3 Common Questions

Where can I find a copyright or trademark character, or a Greek letter?
In the Symbol font.

How do I get a character from the Character Map application into my document?

Select the character by clicking on it. Then click the **Select** button. Then click on the **Copy** button. Paste the character into a word processor like Write (see Chapter 11).

16.4 Details

The Character Map application is very simple to use. There are only four buttons available, one of which is the **Help** button. A combo box lets you select a specific font to view in the window.

16.4.1   The Select Button

The **Select** button copies the currently highlighted character into the **Characters to Copy** text area. From there the character(s) can be copied to the Clipboard with the **Copy** button. You clear the **Characters to Copy** area by dragging over it and pressing the Delete key, or by clicking in it and pressing the Backspace key.

16.4.2   The Copy Button

The **Copy** button copies the contents of the **Characters to Copy** area to the Clipboard. You then paste the Clipboard into another application–generally a word processor like Write–using the normal paste procedure.

16.4.3   The Close Button

The **Close** button exits the Character Map application.

MAIL

17

Depending on your perspective and temperament, electronic mail is either a blessing or a curse. It offers a very convenient way to transmit reports, drawings, and even sound bites to your co-workers. It also reduces phone tag. On the other hand, it tends to depersonalize things and also opens a channel for junk e-mail. A large e-mail system can take on a life of its own. We use e-mail constantly (See Appendix D). Handled with some discretion it can boost your productivity tremendously.

In this chapter you learn how to use the Mail application. This material assumes that you have a Post Office somewhere on your network to which you can connect. Ask your administrator for its location. If there is no Post Office, you may want to consider creating your own. This is described in the Administration book.

17.1 Executive Summary

The Mail application lets you send and receive electronic mail (e-mail) from other NT and Windows for Workgroups users on your network. A central machine acts as a Post Office for all mail messages, and you connect to that Post Office when you want to read or send mail.

The Mail application is shown in Figure 17.1. It offers all the features you'd expect to find in any e-mail system. You can compose new messages, reply to incoming messages, forward mail to other users, and delete old messages. It also contains nice-to-have features such as a personal address book, folders that let you organize your mail, and a "return receipt" capability that notifies you when the recipient has read your message. Finally, it offers a few things that are totally unexpected, such as the ability to create shared folders other e-mail users can examine.

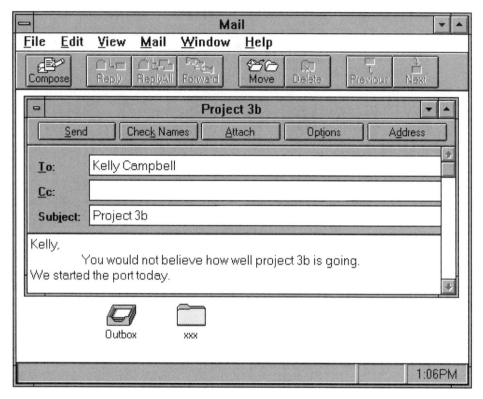

Figure 17.1
The Mail application.

You can send almost anything via e-mail–text, graphics, and sound are all easily incorporated. It's also possible to attach documents–written with Write, for example–to an e-mail message. The attached document appears as an icon embedded in the message and can be read by double-clicking on the icon.

17.2 Guided Tour

To start Mail, double-click on the **Mail** icon in the Main group of the Program Manager. The first time you run the Mail application you see a dialog that asks if you want to connect to an existing Post Office or create a new one. Do not create a new one spontaneously. They take up a good bit of space and, since there's no way to route mail between Post Offices, multiple Post Offices reduce the size of interconnected groups. Ask your administrator or a co-worker for the network path to an existing Post Office.

Once you are connected to the Post Office you need to know your account name and password (depending on the type of Post Office). It's easy to set up the Mail program to log you in automatically (see Section 17.3). Get your account information from the Post Office administrator and type it into the dialog.

17.2.1   Sending a Message

Click on the **Compose** button in the Toolbar or select the **Compose Note** option in the Mail menu. You'll see a Send window similar to the one labeled Project3b in Figure 17.1. This window contains a **To:** field in which you indicate the recipient, a **Cc:** field in which you indicate people to whom copies should be sent, and a subject field. You then begin typing your message in the bottom area. Address this message to yourself (by entering your account name or any unique part of your name) and type something quick in the message area.

There are five buttons in the Send window: **Send, Check Name, Attach, Options**, and **Address**. The **Options** button lets you set the priority of your message and also lets you indicate return receipt notification. When the recipient actually opens the message you receive a post card notifying you of the event if you indicate that you want a return receipt. The **Attach** button lets you attach a file to the e-mail message. The file appears as an icon in the message and can be read by double-clicking on it. The **Check Names** button checks the names in the **To:** and **Cc:** fields. If an invalid name is found, it's tagged and a dialog informs you of the problem. The **Address** button lets you choose names from the list of all users or from your personal Rolodex (see below). Just click on the names and add them to the **To:** or **Cc:** fields. The **Send** button sends the message.

17.2.2   Receiving a Message

Since you sent the message to yourself it ought to arrive shortly. Whenever mail arrives, a small icon appears in the status bar and the application icon itself changes on the desktop if the application is minimized. Look for the **In-**

box icon inside Mail and double-click on it. If you do not see an **Inbox** icon then choose the **Open Inbox** option in the View menu. You should see a window similar to the one shown in Figure 17.2.

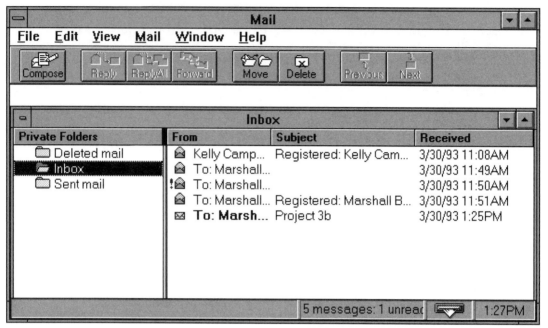

Figure 17.2
The Inbox.

You should have three personal folders in the Inbox initially: One is for mail you have sent, one is for mail you have deleted, and the third is for incoming mail. The **Sent** folder is nice because it keeps a copy of everything you send out (if you don't want the copies, change the check box in the **Mail | Options** option). Double-click on the **Inbox** folder and look for the mail that has arrived. If it hasn't arrived yet then try selecting the **New Messages** option in the View menu. Be patient if it still hasn't arrived because these things take time in a busy Post Office.

Once the message arrives, double-click on its envelope to read its contents. Any envelope marked with an exclamation point is a return receipt message; once you open it the sender knows it. When you're done reading the message you can use the File menu to delete it, print it, or save it to a file. You can also use the **New Folder** option to create a private folder and move or copy it into the folder. For example, if you receive a lot of mail pertaining to a specific project, you can create a folder for that project and place pertinent mail in that folder. You can drag the letter into the new folder or use the **File** options.

It's also possible to reply to a message or forward it to someone else. The **Reply** (reply only to the sender), **Reply to All** (reply to everyone in the **To:** field as well as the sender) and **Forward** options are all in the Mail menu or represented as buttons on the Toolbar. All three of these options create a window that looks just like a Send window. The body of the original message appears at the bottom of the message.

17.2.3 Your Personal Address Book

A large Post Office can have hundreds of users. Selecting names from such a long list can be annoying. Also, you'll tend to have groups of people who always receive messages together. For example, if five people are working together on an engineering problem, then you'll frequently send mail to all five together. Your personal address book solves both of these problems.

Compose a new message and then click the **Address** button in the Send window (see Figure 17.3). If you click on a name and press the **Details** button, you can see all the information known by the Post Office about the user. If you click on a name and then click the **Add** button next to the **Details** button (a Rolodex with a small arrow), the name will be inserted into your Rolodex. You can view the contents of your Rolodex by clicking on the **Rolodex** button (above the magnifying glass, which lets you search the details of all users for a text string). Above the Rolodex is a **Directory** button that lets you switch between your Rolodex and the entire user list.

If you choose the **Mail | Personal Groups** option you can edit and create new groups of users to whom you frequently send mail. Simply click on the **Edit** or **New** button and select and add each name to the group. Each group you create will appear in your personal Rolodex and can be used like any other e-mail address.

17.2.4 Shared Folders

Generally you can place all of your mail in private folders, but there are some occasions where shared folders, viewable by everyone in the Post Office, are useful. For example, you might create a shared folder that holds conference announcements, or another one to act like a community bulletin board.

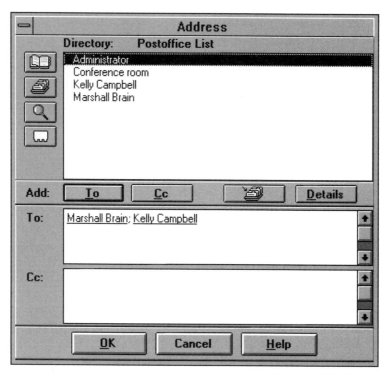

Figure 17.3
The Address list.

To create a shared folder choose the **New Folder** option in the File menu. Click the **Shared Radio** button. You can now flip your **Inbox** display between private and shared folders. Use the **Copy** and **Move** options in the File menu to fill the folder. Use the **Folder Properties** option in the File menu to control access to the shared folder.

17.2.5   The Clipboard

Mail is an OLE client (see Chapter 10 for a description of this concept if you are unfamiliar with it). If you copy something onto the clipboard from an OLE server like Paintbrush (see Chapter 9), then you can embed the object directly into the e-mail message. Using the **Attach** button in the Send window you can also attach files to an e-mail message. Any type of file can be attached and it will appear as an icon in the e-mail message. The **File | Save Attachment** option lets you save the attached files from a letter you receive.

17.3 Common Questions

? *How do I make Mail start automatically when I log in to NT?*
Copy the **Mail** icon in the Main group of the Program Manager into the Start-up group (see Chapter 2). If you want the icon to automatically log you in as well, select the icon, choose the **Properties** option in the File menu, and add your user name and password to the command line (e.g., "MSMAIL32.EXE brain passwd"). Do not use this feature unless you're certain your account and its file system are secure. This auto log in feature will not work with a null password.

? *How do I send an e-mail message?*
Click the **Compose** button or choose the **Compose Note** option in the Mail menu.

? *How do I send mail to a group of users?*
Enter the names, separated by semicolons, in the **To:** field of the Send window. You can also create personal groups if you frequently send mail to the same set of people (see Section 17.2.4).

? *How do I send mail return receipt?*
In the Send window, click the **Options** button and select the **Return Receipt** check box.

? *How do I change the font?*
Use the **Change Font** option in the View menu.

? *How do I send a picture?*
You can copy it to the Clipboard and then paste it into the message, or save it in a file and attach the file to the letter. Any type of file can be attached to an e-mail message.

? *I have this return receipt letter and I don't want to acknowledge the sender's presence. What can I do?*
Select the message with a single-click and delete it with the **File | Delete** option.

? *How do I copy a letter into a shared folder?*
Select the letter and choose the **File | Copy** option.

? *How do I make the Inbox display my messages rather than the shared folders?*
Choose the **View | Private Folders** option.

? *How do I look at received mail?*
Double-click on the **Inbox** icon. If you cannot find it, use the **View |**
Open Inbox option.

? *How do I extract an attached file from a message?*
View the message and select the **File | Save Attachment** option.

17.4 Details

17.4.1 The File Menu

This menu lets you manipulate mail messages and folders.

17.4.1.1 The File | Open Option

This option opens the selected folder or message. Alternately, you can
double-click on either.

17.4.1.2 The File | Move Option

This option moves the selected message or folder into the referenced folder. Alternately, you can drag the message into a private folder.

17.4.1.3 The File | Copy Option

This option copies the selected message into the referenced folder.

17.4.1.4 The File | Delete Option

This option deletes the selected message or folder. Alternately, you can
drag the item into the **Deleted Mail** folder.

17.4.1.5 The File | Save As Option

This option saves the selected message to a file.

17.4.1.6 The File | Save Attachment Option

This option saves attachments within the current message to separate files.
The default name for each file is the original name of the file.

17.4.1.7   The File | Message Finder Option

This option helps you to find specific messages. You can search on the sender, the subject, the recipients, or the body of the message.

17.4.1.8   The File | New Folder Option

This option is used to create new private or shared folders.

17.4.1.9   The File | Folder Properties Option

This option lets you change the properties of a private or shared folder. If it's a shared folder, you control user permissions on it with this option.

17.4.1.10   The File | Export Folder Option

The **Export** option lets you export one or more of your folders to a disk file. The file can later be read in using the **Import** option.

17.4.1.11   The File | Import Folder Option

This option lets you read in a file saved by the previous option.

17.4.1.12   The File | Print Option

This option prints the currently selected message to the default printer.

17.4.1.13   The File | Print Setup Option

This option lets you select the default printer and tune its behavior.

17.4.1.14   The File | Exit Option

This option exits the Mail application but leaves the reminder program running so you're reminded of appointments (see Chapter 12).

17.4.1.15   The File | Exit and Sign Out Option

This option exits the Mail application and terminates the reminder program.

17.4.2   The Edit Menu

This menu allows you to move data between the Clipboard and your e-mail messages.

17.4.2.1   The Edit | Undo Option

This option undoes the previous action.

17.4.2.2   The Edit | Cut Option

This option cuts the currently selected portion of the document to the Clipboard. The selection can then be pasted into other documents.

17.4.2.3   The Edit | Copy Option

This option copies the currently selected portion of the document to the Clipboard. The selection can then be pasted into other documents.

17.4.2.4   The Edit | Paste Option

This option pastes the contents of the Clipboard into the current document. If the Clipboard entry was placed there by an OLE server, then the object will be embedded (and can be edited by double-clicking on it in the document). If not, it will simply be pasted.

17.4.2.5   The Edit | Paste Special Option

This option is only available if the current selection on the Clipboard was placed there by an OLE server such as Paintbrush (see Chapter 9). You will see a dialog that displays the different formats in which the data was placed on the Clipboard, and several buttons. If you click the **Paste** button the selection is embedded (this button is equivalent to the **Paste** option in the Edit menu).

17.4.2.6   The Edit | Delete Option

This option deletes the current selection.

17.4.2.7   The Edit | Select All Option

This option selects the entire message.

17.4.2.8   The Edit | Edit ... Object Option

This option allows you to modify an embedded object. An alternative is to double-click on the object.

17.4.2.9   The Edit | Insert Object Option

This option allows you to embed a new object of the specified type. The appropriate application will execute and you create the new object in it.

17.4.2.10   The Edit | Insert From File Option

This option inserts the contents of the selected file into the current message. Generally this option should be used only for text files. For other types of files, attach them using the **Attach** button in the **Send** window.

17.4.3   The View Menu

This menu lets you change your view of the current messages and folders. The menu changes depending on whether the focused window is the Inbox, a received message, or a Send window. If it is a Send window, you can change the font used to display the message with the **Change Font**. If it is a received message you can move to the next or previous message. If the window is the Inbox, the following options apply.

17.4.3.1   The View | Shared Folders Option

This option changes the Inbox from viewing personal folders to viewing shared folders.

17.4.3.2   The View | New Messages Option

This option forces new messages into the Inbox. Messages are normally read from the Post Office on an interval set in the Options dialog.

17.4.3.3   The View | Sort by Sender Option

This option sorts messages by sender in the currently displayed folder.

17.4.3.4   The View | Sort by Subject Option

This option sorts messages by subject in the currently displayed folder.

17.4.3.5   The View | Sort by Date Option

This option sorts messages by date in the currently displayed folder.

17.4.3.6   The View | Sort by Priority Option

This option sorts messages by priority in the currently displayed folder.

17.4.3.7   The View | Tool Bar Option

This option toggles the Toolbar on and off.

17.4.3.8   The View | Status Bar Option

This option toggles the Status bar on and off.

17.4.4   The Mail Menu

This menu lets you send and reply to mail.

17.4.4.1   The Mail | Compose Note Option

This option lets you compose a new message. A Send window will appear that allows you to specify the recipients and the contents of the messages (see Section 17.2.1 for an example).

17.4.4.2   The Mail | Reply Option

This option lets you reply to the selected message in the Inbox. It replies only to the original sender (see Section 17.2.2 for an example).

17.4.4.3   The Mail | Reply to All Option

This option lets you reply to the selected message in the Inbox. It replies to the sender and everyone in the **To:** list (see section 17.2.2 for an example).

17.4.4.4   The Mail | Forward Option

This option lets you forward the current message to another recipient (see section 17.2.2 for an example).

17.4.4.5   The Mail | Address Book Option

This message lets you manipulate your address book (see Section 17.2.3 for an example).

17.4.4.6   The Mail | Personal Groups Option

This option lets you add a personal group to your address book. A personal group is a collection of recipients to whom you commonly send particular types of mail. For example, you might typically send purchasing questions to a collection of three people in the purchasing department. You can form a group that contains those three people and save yourself having to type their names every time you send a message. The group lives in your address book (see Section 17.2.3 for an example).

17.4.4.7   The Mail | Options Option

This option lets you control the behavior of the Mail application. You can specify the following behaviors:

- Saving of outgoing messages
- Automatic addition of recipients to your address book
- Mail reading interval from the Post Office
- Mail arrival behavior
- Deletion of mail upon exit

17.4.4.8   The Mail | Change Password Option

This option lets you change your Post Office password. This password affects both this application and Schedule+ (see Chapter 12).

17.4.4.9   The Mail | Backup Option

This option backs up your current message folders and messages to an external file.

Chat

The Mail application in Chapter 17 emulates the postal system. Chat emulates the phone company. Chat lets you form an immediate face-to-face, or in this case finger-to-finger, connection with another person on the network.

18.1 Executive Summary

The Chat application lets you connect to another workstation over the network and type messages back and forth to whoever is logged in at the time. Figure 18.1 shows a typical Chat window. Whatever you type in the upper window is echoed in the lower window on the recipient's screen, and vice versa.

Chat is more of a novelty than anything else. If there's a phone available it's a whole lot quicker and easier to use. If no phone's available, however, Chat can be useful–and it's quicker than e-mail.

18.2 Guided Tour

Start the Chat application by double-clicking on its icon in the Accessories group of the Program Manager. Choose the **Dial** option in the Conversation menu. You will see a dialog box listing all the available connection points on the network. If there are none then you should be able to connect to yourself.

Figure 18.1
The Chat application.

The recipient of your attempt at connection will hear a sound (a beep or synthesized ringing, depending on the hardware). The **Chat** icon will also appear and animate itself. The recipient can double-click on the **Chat** icon to answer the call. Once a connection has been established, anything you type will be transmitted to the recipient and anything the recipient types will appear on your screen.

If the recipient already has the Chat window visible, then the ringing sound will play and the recipient needs to choose the **Answer** option from the Conversation menu.

When you are done with the conversation, choose **Hangup** in the Conversation menu.

Select the **Preferences** option in the Options menu. You can specify the window arrangement (horizontal or vertical) and the font preference. You can also control the colors, font, sound, Toolbar, and status line from the Options menu.

The Clipboard makes it easy to move text from other applications into your Chat window and send it along to the recipient. This isn't so easy to do with a telephone.

18.3 Common Questions

I hear this peculiar double beep noise or ringing noise from my machine. What is it?
Someone is trying to form a Chat connection to you. Find the **Chat** icon and double-click on it to form a connection.

What if I don't want to chat?
Turn off the sound in the Options menu.

18.4 Details

18.4.1 The Conversation Menu

This menu lets you establish a connection with another user.

18.4.1.1 The Conversation | Dial Option

This option presents a dialog that lets you choose the recipient on the network.

18.4.1.2 The Conversation | Answer Option

This option lets you answer a call being placed from another machine.

18.4.1.3 The Conversation | Hang Up Option

This option hangs up the current call and breaks the connection.

18.4.1.4 The Conversation | Exit Option

This option terminates the Chat application and hangs up on the current connection. If another user tries to call, Chat will start automatically in a minimized state.

18.4.2 The Edit Menu

This menu lets you move information on and off the Clipboard.

·18.4.2.1   The Edit | Cut Option

This option cuts the current selection from the Chat window and places it on the Clipboard.

18.4.2.2   The Edit | Copy Option

This option copies the current selection onto the Clipboard.

18.4.2.3   The Edit | Paste Option

This option pastes the text on the Clipboard into your Chat window and transmits it to the recipient.

18.4.2.4   The Edit | Select All Option

This option selects everything in your window.

18.4.3   The Options Menu

This menu lets you adjust the behavior of the Chat application.

18.4.3.1   The Options | Preferences Option

This option presents a dialog that lets you modify the window orientation and the font choice.

18.4.3.2   The Options | Font Option

This option changes the font used in your copy of Chat. If the recipient chooses it in the preferences dialog, that font choice is reflected in their window as well.

18.4.3.3   The Options | Background Color Option

This option modifies the background color.

18.4.3.4   The Options | Toolbar Option

This option toggles the Toolbar on and off.

18.4.3.5   The Options | Status Bar Option

This option toggles the status line on and off.

18.4.3.6   The Options | Sound Option

This option toggles sound on and off.

So, You've Never Seen a Mouse Before...

A

If this is the first time you've seen or used a mouse, then we know how you feel right now. You pick up this thing that looks like a bar of soap with a couple of buttons on it and you ask yourself, "*This* is an input device?" When you try to use it you feel clumsy, and you aren't exactly sure what you're supposed to do with it. That's OK. Just go shut your door for ten minutes so nobody has to watch. Soon, very soon, you'll be a pro.

The goal of this appendix is to teach you how to use a mouse. You will learn basic mouse vocabulary and the different techniques used to manipulate objects. You will also learn about the basic controls found in Windows NT—buttons, scroll bars, combo boxes, and such—so you know how to use them. Once you have been properly introduced, it will take a day or so for you to get completely comfortable with your mouse. But then you will begin to use it automatically and you won't think about it again.

Before you can use your mouse you have to log in to Windows NT. The log in procedure is described in Chapter 1, but let's go through it here in slow motion. If this is your first time logging in then the procedure may seem like a lot of work, especially if there are problems. After you've done it a few times, however, you should feel comfortable with it. Here are the steps:

1.   If the machine is off, turn it on.

2.   Figure out your user log in and password. Ask the system administrator or the person who installed NT for you to give you this account information.

3.   Once the machine is on and "up," you should see a small box that says "Press CTRL+ALT+DEL to log on." If you don't see this box, it probably means that the last user forgot to log out. Ask your system administrator or the person who installed NT for help. Generally, it's a bad idea to turn the machine off and then back on, or to hit the reset button. You might erase data that the last user hasn't saved yet.

4.   Look on the keyboard and find a key marked "Ctrl," one marked "Alt," and one marked "Del." There are generally two sets of these keys, and it doesn't matter which set you choose. Press all three simultaneously.

5.   You will see the "Welcome dialog," as shown in Figure A.1. This dialog lets you *log in*. By logging in you identify yourself to the computer. Find the Tab key and press it a few times. Watch what happens. This is called *moving the focus*. The *focus*, or the *keyboard focus,* is the area of the screen that is going to receive any input from the keyboard. Using the Tab key, move the focus up to the Username field (it rotates back to the top when you hit the bottom). Type in your user name (ask your system administrator if you are unsure).

6.   Press the tab key so that the Password field has focus (ignore the Domain field). Type your password (again, ask your administrator). Press the Enter key and you will be logged in. If your log in is rejected you will see a message telling you that the user name or password you typed is incorrect. Try again. If you are rejected several times, ask for help.

7.   You may receive a message telling you that the system is having problems making a connection. Hit the **N** key to tell the system you do not want it to continue.

8.   Now you are logged in.

It's hard to say exactly what you'll see on your screen because the administrator for your system may have configured it in a different way. What we need to do is get you to a known point so we can continue. Look at your screen. There are three possible things you'll see:

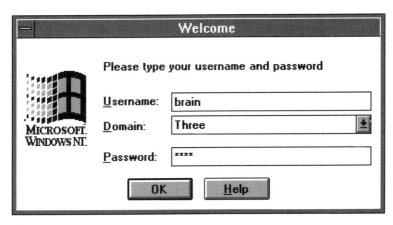

Figure A.1
The Welcome dialog.

1. The screen has a *background* (also called wallpaper) that appears on the screen at all times. It may get covered over by other windows, but once all those windows are removed you see the background again. What we want to do right now is *minimize* all the windows so that we can see the background.

2. The screen may also contain *icons,* which are small pictures arranged at the bottom of the screen. When an application is *minimized,* it appears as an icon. We want all the applications minimized like this.

3. The screen probably has one or more *windows* visible. A window is the working area for an application. If all that you see is background and icons, then you do not need to do anything. If you see windows then you need to minimize them. Along the top of any window is a bar called the *Title Bar.* On the left side of the Title Bar is a small square called the *System menu.* Press the Alternate key and while it's down press the space bar. This action will pull down the System menu's items. Press the down arrow key until the word **Minimize** is highlighted. (If the system beeps when you press the down arrow key, look for a second down arrow key on the keyboard and use it instead, or find the key labeled **Num Lock,** press it, and try the arrow key again.) Once the **Minimize** item is highlighted, press the Enter key. If the menu does not contain the word **Minimize,** select the word **Close** instead. Do this until all the windows are minimized and displayed as icons at the bottom of the screen. All you should see when you get done are icons and the background.

Now you can learn how to use the mouse. Grab the mouse and look at it. It probably has two or three buttons on the top. The only button that matters to us right now is the left-most button. Turn the mouse over. You will probably see a ball, or maybe two small disks. When you move the mouse on your table or desk, the ball or disks move and the mouse sends movement signals to the computer so the computer can move the arrow on screen.

In order to use a mouse effectively, you have to learn how to do four things: moving, clicking, double-clicking, and dragging. Once you can do all four then you are an experienced mouse user. Let's start with moving the mouse.

Move the mouse around on your table or desk and watch the screen. There is an arrow on the screen that follows the mouse's motion. The arrow is called the *cursor*. Touch all four corners of the screen with the cursor. Notice that the cursor never leaves the screen, but it can become almost invisible at the bottom and right sides of the screen. You may find that your desk is not big enough–you cannot move the mouse far enough to traverse the entire screen. If this happens, pick the mouse up and move it. Then put it back down and continue moving the cursor (if that sentence doesn't make sense, take it literally and do what it says. Pick the mouse up. While it is in the air, move it. Put it back down and move the cursor some more–you will see what is happening in a moment and then be able to traverse the whole screen).

Now move the cursor so the tip of the arrow is touching the middle of the icon labeled "Program Manager." *Click* the left mouse button. That is, push it down and release it with your forefinger. (If you are a lefty and the mouse is in your left hand this is going to be awkward. You will see how to reverse the mouse buttons in Chapter 3.) You should see a little *menu* pop up. A menu contains a list of options. Now move the cursor to the side of the icon, so the tip of the cursor is touching the background, and click on the background. The menu will go away. Repeat these steps a few times.

Now click on the **Program Manager** icon again so that the menu appears. Move the cursor so the tip of the arrow is touching the middle of one of the letters in the word **Restore**. Click on this word. The window will appear. Now minimize the window again. Since you know how to click you now have three ways to minimize a window:

1. Use the **Alt-space bar** combination and the down arrow key to select **Minimize** in the menu and then press return.

2. Each window has a *Title Bar* along the top. Click on the small down-pointing arrow (a down-pointing triangle, actually) on the right side of the Title Bar.

3. Click on the System menu square at the left side of the Title Bar, and then click on the word **Minimize** in the menu.

Try all three techniques several times. Also try *maximizing* the window by clicking on the small upward-pointing arrow. The application will enlarge to fill the entire screen, and the upward-pointing arrow changes to a double arrow. Click on the double arrow to return the window to its normal size. Practice this operation until you are comfortable. Then return the screen to its original state where everything is minimized.

Now move the cursor onto the **Program Manager** icon again. Instead of clicking on it once and selecting **Restore,** *double-click* on it. To double-click something, you click on it twice in rapid succession. This takes a little getting used to. You have to click it twice in about a tenth of a second or so, and *you cannot move the mouse between the two clicks*. It will probably take you several tries but, when you successfully double-click on the icon, the window will restore itself. Practice double-clicking the icon to restore the window and then minimize the window with a single-click on the minimize button. Do this several times until you feel comfortable with the process.

The last mouse action you need to learn is called *dragging*. You normally drag something to move it to a different location on the screen. Move the cursor onto the **Program Manager** icon. Now click the left mouse button down and, *without releasing it*, move the mouse around. The icon will move with the cursor until you release the mouse button. Now move the icon back to where it was.

Restore the Program Manager window to its normal size by double-clicking on its icon. You can move the window (provided it is not maximized) by dragging it with the Title Bar. Move the cursor onto the word "Program" in the Title Bar, push the mouse button down and hold it while you move the mouse. An outline will follow the cursor and, when you release the mouse button, the window will move.

You *re-size* a window by dragging one of its edges. As an example, move the cursor slowly until the tip of the arrow touches the left edge of the window. When the cursor changes to a double arrow, drag the edge to the right and the window will re-size. This also works in the corners of the window. Practice re-sizing and moving the window several times. Notice also that double-clicking on the Title Bar maximizes the window, and double-clicking on it again returns the window to its original size.

Now you are an experienced mouse user. You know how to move the mouse, how to click on objects to select them, how to drag objects to move them, and how to double-click on icons and the Title Bar. Here are the vocabulary words we covered. If any seem unfamiliar, review the material in this Appendix:

background
click
double-click
drag
icon
maximize
minimize
move
restore
System menu
Title Bar
window

Here are a few more useful words:

- Menu Bar: The area just below the Title Bar in most windows. In the Program Manager window, the Menu Bar contains the words "File," "Options," and so on.

- Menu: The individual elements in a Menu Bar. For example, if you click on the word "File" in the Program Manager's Menu bar, the File menu will appear. To get rid of the menu, click on the background, or on the white area at the end of the Menu Bar, or press the **Esc** (Escape) key twice.

- Button: An area that accepts single-clicks to perform a specified action. For example, when you single-click on the minimize button of the Title Bar, the window minimizes.

- Scroll Bar: A long thin control that lets you move around a document or large application screen. Figure A.2 and A.3 show scroll bars. You can click on the arrows of a scroll bar, or on the shaft of the scroll bar. In a text document these actions are the same as the arrow keys and the Page Up and Page Down keys. You can also drag the box in the shaft to move to a specific location.

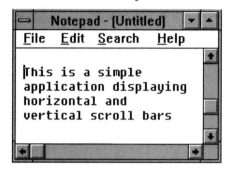

Figure A.2
Scroll bars in an application.

Figure A.3
Parts of a scroll bar.

- Dialog Box: Look at the File menu for the Program Manager. Near the bottom of the menu is the **Logoff** option. Click on the word **Logoff**. A *dialog box* will appear asking you if you are sure you want to log off. If you are, click on the OK button. If you do not want to log off, click on the Cancel button. In some cases there will be an under-lined letter on the button's label. If there is, you can type that letter on the keyboard in lieu of clicking the button.
- Edit area: An edit area lets you enter text. Once the edit area has the focus (click on the edit area or use the Tab key to get the focus), you can type in it with the keyboard. You can move the cursor with the mouse or arrow keys. Delete characters with the Delete or Backspace keys. You can also drag over areas of text with the mouse (or hold down the Shift key and use the arrow keys) to select a group of characters and then delete them. Figure A.4 shows a typical edit area.
- List: A list displays a collection of strings and allows you to choose one either by single-clicking it and then clicking a button or by double-clicking on an item in the list. Some lists will let you choose multiple items by holding down the Shift key and clicking on an item. A typical list is shown in Figure A.5.

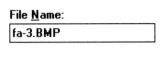

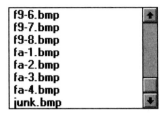

Figure A.4
A typical edit area.

Figure A.5
A typical list.

- Combo Box: A combo box combines an editable area with a list. Click on the arrow to expand the list portion of the combo box. See Figures A.6 and A.7 for pictures of a combo box and an expanded combo box. Combo boxes are used in applications because they save space on the screen. Only when the list is needed is it visible.

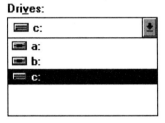

Figure A.6
A combo box in its small configuration.

Figure A.7
A combo box with its list visible.

Play around with the mouse until you are comfortable with it. In a short time its use will become completely automatic.

When you are ready, log off and turn to Chapter 1. To log off, press the Ctrl-Alt-Del triplet and click on the **Logoff** button.

INSTALLING WINDOWS NT

B

Windows NT is available for several machine architectures and has a huge number of installation options. You will need to read the Microsoft documentation to perform the install. If you choose the express setup, then your decisions are minimized and the whole process is relatively straightforward.

Installation on a PC is probably, and ironically, the most difficult because of the millions of possible machine configurations. On a workstation, NT can make a huge number of assumptions about the hardware, and the user will almost certainly be creating a "pure NT machine"–a machine that runs only NT. If you are installing on a PC you have several decisions you need to make before starting the install:

1. Do you want a pure NT machine, or one that can boot both NT and DOS?
2. Do you want your hard disk formatted for the FAT file system or the NT file system? If the machine can swap between DOS and NT then the DOS partition will have to remain a FAT partition. You can format your other partitions and drives with the NT file system, however. If you do, the partitions will become invisible to DOS, so there is a trade-off. There is a definite convenience factor to being able to see all files from both DOS and NT. On the other hand, the NT file system partitions will be more secure and robust.
3. Will your machine reside on a network? If so, you need to find out what kind of network card you have and get NT drivers for it if NT does not ship with those drivers.

Special pieces of hardware may **also need** NT drivers. You will have to acquire them from the manufacturer.

The installation program will **create an** *administrator account* on the machine, and it will give you the opportunity **to create** a user account as well. This user account will need some tuning later (see Appendix C). The administration account is used to administer **the machine, and it** gives you the power to do anything you want at any time. That **power includes** the ability to make the machine totally non-functional. **You will want to** use the administration account only occasionally, **and when necessary to perform** specific administration tasks. You should use the user account **at all other** times. See Appendix C for more information on the differences **between** administration and user accounts.

ADMINISTRATION BASICS

This book is not about administration. There is an entirely separate book on that subject in this series. Administration is a rather large topic, especially on big corporate networks, and it can get extremely complicated.

But what if you have a lone NT machine at your office, or two or three machines in your department networked together? You will have to *administer* those machines. That is, you will have to log in as the Administrator and perform certain tasks such as:

1. Creating user accounts. For example, if a friend needs to use your machine you will have to create a separate account for him or her.
2. Changing your own privileges and customizing your account.
3. Modifying virtual memory.
4. Sharing drives on the network.
5. Changing the time and date.
6. Adding drivers for equipment and new printers.
7. Formatting hard drives.
8. Installing new software.

For all of these tasks you need a basic understanding of the Administrator's role and you need to understand why accounts are important. This chapter will introduce you to these topics and show you how to perform standard administration tasks.

219

C.1 What Are Accounts and Who Is the Administrator?

When NT installs itself, it creates two accounts: The Administrator account and a user account. If you have never had to "log in" to a machine before you may be asking yourself, "Why do we need accounts at all? My DOS machine never had accounts and it works just fine." The idea of accounts, in combination with a secure file system like the NT file system, combines to create a secure system. Accounts by themselves do not create security because anyone who logs in can look at all the files. Secure files without accounts do not work because there is no way to identify who should be able to look at the secure files. No one would be able to look at anything.

When you have both accounts and a secure file system, the system is secure. When a person logs in to an account the operating system knows exactly who that person is. If the person has been careful with his or her password, only that one person can get into the account. If the file system allows the users to specify exactly who can see certain files, then a person who logs in will only be able to access the files to which they have permission. This level of security gives all users private workspaces that cannot be breached unless users give permissions to each other.

NT can be a secure system. It always has accounts and, if your hard disk is formatted with the NT file system, it becomes secure. Therefore, even if your NT machine is sitting in your living room and you are the only one who ever uses it, it will be secure. You can use this technology to your advantage. For example, if you want to let the kids use the machine to play Tetris, you can give them a separate account and limit their access to just one file in one directory if you like. They will not be able to touch anything else on the entire system, so you won't have to worry about them messing anything up. If you have a machine in your office you can create an account for a co-worker. That person can use the machine at night and work only in one directory. The rest of your data is completely secure and you don't have to worry about anything, short of a Coke spilled on the keyboard.

There are certain parts of the operating system to which no normal user should have access. For example, no normal user needs to be able to see the operating system files. No normal user needs to be able to erase the virtual memory paging file. No normal user needs to be able to move DLL files for an application. If users are able to do things to the operating system or applications, then it's likely that something will get broken in the process. For good reason those parts of the hard disk are locked away. On occasion someone needs to get to them to upgrade the operating system, for example, or to add a device driver, or to install a new application. The power to perform these tasks is given to a special account called the Administrator account.

Every NT machine has an Administrator account. The Administrator can do anything anywhere. The Administrator can look at any file, in any directory, regardless of permissions set for those files. Therefore the Administrator can do anything he or she wants.

This should tell you one thing: You don't want just anyone to be able to log in as the Administrator on your machine. If they can, then they have the power to destroy it. If you are working in a big company, *you* may not even be able to log in as the Administrator on your machine. There may be a whole department in the company whose job is administration, and you are simply a user. It also tells you something else: As a general rule you do not want to log in as Administrator unless you need all of those privileges. If you are always logged in as a user, it's impossible to do anything that breaks the operating system.

If you own your machine, then you will occasionally have to log in as the Administrator to administer your system. The following sections list the common tasks you perform.

C.2 Users, Groups, and File Permissions

In order to administer a system you have to understand three concepts: accounts, groups, and files. In this context we are going to consider files and directories to be equivalent entities on the disk.

An account identifies a user. When you log into your account you identify yourself to the operating system. Your account also stores all your personal preferences. Your desktop colors, wallpaper selection, application defaults, and so on are all stored with your account so each user can have their own settings.

A group identifies a collection of users, as well as a collection of privileges. An account gets its privileges from the group(s) of which it is a member. For example, if you are a member of the "Users" group, you have the right to log in, to use the system, and to shut down the system. That's about it. You do not have the right to change the system time, or to install device drivers. It's possible to create custom groups, however. For example, you might create a group called "Programmers" that has special rights. All the users who need those rights would be members of the group. It's also possible for a user to be a member of several groups.

Files use both accounts and groups to grant access. For example, an individual file or directory is owned by one specific user. That user can set permissions on the file or directory that allow certain users to access the file, or that allow certain groups of users to access the file. For example, a code directory needs to be accessed by all programmers, so members of the Programmers group can be given access to the directory. Chapter 5 discusses file access privileges.

C.3 Customizing Your Personal Account

The first time you log in you will want to log in as the Administrator to customize your personal user account. This account should have been created when NT was installed. There are two things about your account that you can change: your user privileges and your environment profile. Once you get your user account arranged to your liking, you will use it for all your normal work.

Log in as the Administrator and find the Administrative Tools group in the Program Manager. Double-click on the User Manager tool in that group. You will see a dialog similar to the one shown in Figure C.1. This dialog is used to create new accounts and manage existing accounts. It lists all the user accounts on your machine along with all the groups that are defined.

A group collects together a specific set of user privileges, and also names a set of users. Each user is a member of at least one group, but can be a member of many. The Administrator can create new groups. For example, a group of programmers working on a specific project might be members of the "programmer" group. Files are accessed on a per-user or a per-group basis.

If you want to give yourself more privileges, you have two choices: You can change your group to "Power User," which is just a notch below Administrator, or you can create a new group and give it the privileges you want. To create the new group use the **New Local Group** option in the User menu and give it a name (or select an existing group and **Copy** it). Then use the **User Rights** option in the **Policies** menu to determine the exact rights it has. Select specific rights from the Rights combo box and **Add** them.

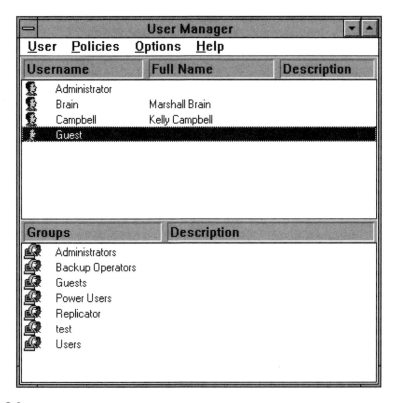

Figure C.1
The User Manager.

Now double-click on your account in the Users list. You will see a dialog similar to the one shown in Figure C.2. Click on the **Groups** button. You can add and remove yourself from certain groups. If you click on the **Profile** button you will see a dialog similar to Figure C.3. In this dialog you can:

1. Set up a batch file that is executed every time you log on.
2. Establish a "home directory."

Your home directory is the default directory that all applications use when they are launched from the Program Manager with no Working Directory specified. You can create your user directory anywhere in the directory tree, but it's generally considered a good idea to locate user directories in a common place, such as a directory named "users" off the root directory. NT creates this directory for you automatically, so you should use it. Create yourself a home directory in the "users" directory and then set the local path to that directory

in the dialog. Also, be sure to check the permissions on the directory using the
File Manager. You need to give your user account access to your home directory while you are the Administrator (see Chapter 5). The Drive Connections
can be specified much more easily in the File Manager, so you probably want
to do it there (see Chapter 5).

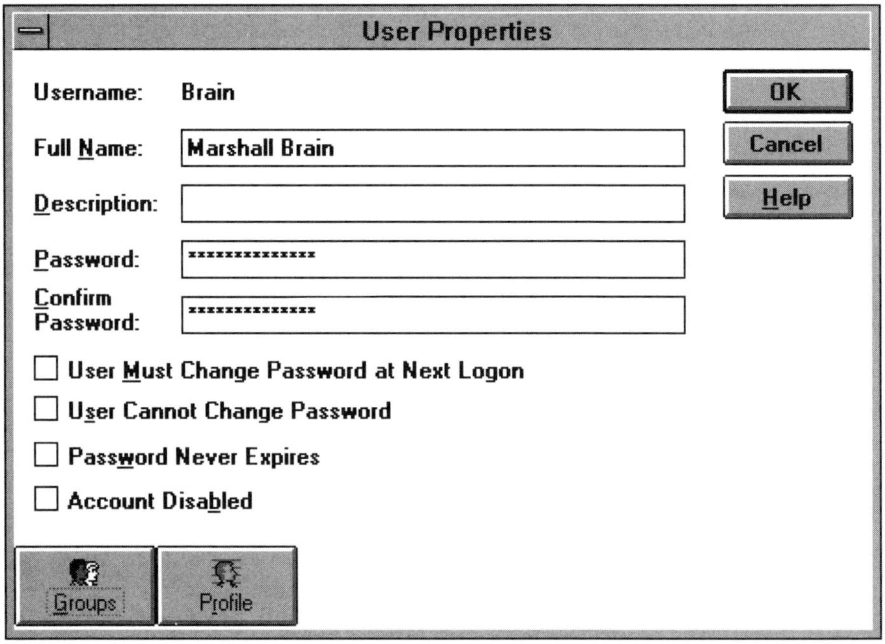

Figure C.2
The User Properties dialog.

C.4 Creating a New User

If you want to give other people access to your NT machine, the best way
to do it is to create new accounts for them. That way they will be able to work
in their own workspaces without having access to the rest of the system. They
also will be able to set their own preferences without changing anyone else's.
To add a new account you must do the following:

1.   Create the new account in the User Manager. Double-click on the **User
     Manager** icon in the Administrative Tools group of the Program Man-
     ager. Select the **New User** option in the User menu. Enter the User

Name (the log in name that the user will type in the Welcome dialog), the user's full name, a description (be nice), and the starting password.

2. Add the new account to one or more groups using the **Groups** button at the bottom of the New User dialog. The "Users" group is a safe one if you have no preference and haven't created your own custom groups. "Guests" is also a good group that has fewer privileges than "Users."

3. Create the user's home directory. A good place for this directory is the "users" directory created by NT. Use the File Manager to search for "users" if you cannot find it, and then create a new directory there. Set the new user's home directory by clicking on the **Profile** button in the New User dialog.

4. Change the permissions on the new home directory so that the new account you have created has access (see Chapter 5).

5. If desired, create a Logon Script (a batch file) that executes whenever the user logs in.

Now the new user can log in and work in his or her home directory without disturbing anyone.

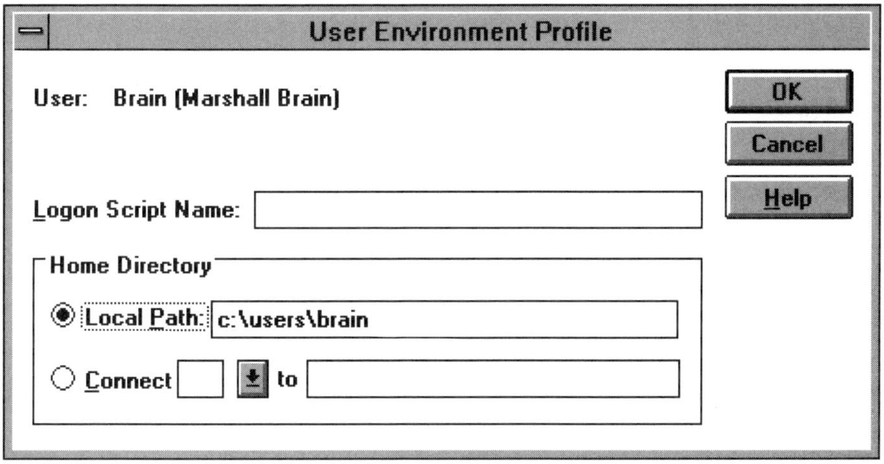

Figure C.3
The User Environment Profile dialog.

C.5 Sharing Drives

One of your most important tasks as an Administrator will be to share drives on your system with others over the network. Read Chapter 5 for a discussion of drive and directory sharing.

C.6 Use of the Control Panel and Program Manager

There are many applets in the Control Panel (Chapter 3) that can only be used by the Administrator. The two most commonly used are **System** and **Time & Date**. The latter is pretty obvious once you see the applet. Click on a segment (the month, the hour, etc.) and then either type over it or click on the small arrows to change the values. The **System** applet contains a **Virtual Memory** button that lets you modify your page file size and location.

As the Administrator, you can also create "Common Program Groups" in the Program Manager. Normal users can create their own personal groups of icons, but as the Administrator you can create groups that appear in everyone's Program Manager. When you install a new application, create a new common group for it.

C.7 Other Administrative Tasks

There are several other common administrative tasks you'll routinely perform. For example, you should switch over to Administrator mode whenever you install new software. This will allow you to put the software anywhere and give its directories their proper permissions.

All device driver changes must be performed by the Administrator. As the Administrator you can use the **Windows NT Setup** application in the Main group of the Program Manager. The most likely reason to use this application is to change your screen driver. Choose the **Change System Settings** option in the Options menu and then select an existing display driver from the list, or select "other" and supply a new driver on a floppy. When you install a new printer on your machine, you will want to use the **Create Printer** option in the Printer menu of the Print Manager to select its driver or install a new one.

Be sure to keep your Administrator password secure. Don't give it out. Frequent changes are also advised. See the section on password changing in Chapter 1.

C.8 Conclusion

When it comes time to add new drives, connect your machine on the network and hook up to TCP/IP machines on the net. Here, you begin to leave the realm of simple administration and enter the territory called "real" administration. At that point you will need to get the administration book and start to become an expert.

CONTACTING THE AUTHORS

Windows NT, like all operating systems, will change over time. We want to keep your copy of the book current by providing you with correction and update pages via electronic mail. If you find errors in the book, or if you have any questions, comments, or suggestions for improving the book, we would like to hear from you. Your comments will help us improve later editions, and we'll post your corrections so other readers can take advantage of them.

You can contact the authors either by U.S. mail or by electronic mail. Electronic mail is preferred. The U.S. mail address is:

Interface Technologies
P.O. Box 841
Zebulon, NC 27597

To send suggestions, comments, or corrections via electronic mail, address e-mail to:

comments@iftech.com

To ask a question, send e-mail to:

questions@iftech.com

To request a list of the available update and correction pages, as well as supplements, send e-mail to:

info@iftech.com

In the last case, the message can contain anything or nothing at all. The mail system will send an automated reply with a list of topics and further instructions.

These e-mail addresses are on the Internet and will suffice on mail systems connected directly to the Internet. If you are using Compuserve, you can add the prefix "INTERNET:" to the address to get your message onto the Internet. For example:

```
INTERNET:comments@iftech.com
```

Other mail services such as MCImail, as well as many PC bulletin boards, also offer Internet access. See the documentation for your specific system for details.

INDEX

Symbols

90
%0 95, 98
%1 94, 98
& 90
&& 88
* 51, 91
. 43, 91
*.txt 43, 45, 51
. (one dot) 38, 39
.login 89
.. (two dots) 38, 39
> 93
? 45, 51, 92
??.bmp 52
@ 96
| 93
|| 88

A

access 65
  bits
    change permissions
      65
    delete 65
    execute 65
    read 65
    take ownership 65
    write 65
  network 67
  No Access permissions
    67
  special 66
accessories group 14
accounts 6
  administrator 220
  customizing 222
  user 220
add option 178
address book option 195,
  202
administration group 14
administrator 14, 68
alarm clock 101
alarms 160
alias 89
all file details option 43, 56
allocation problems 101
Alt-PrtSc 119
Alt-Tab key 14, 15, 32
always on top option 181

Amiga 2
analog option 180
answer option 206
application
  opening 20
  running 14, 20, 21
  starting 14, 20
application groups in the
  Program Manager 13
application icon 13
arrange icons option 59, 80
associate option 45, 51
AT command 101
attached files 196
ATTRIB command 101
auditing option 80
authors
  contacting 228
Auto Arrange 22
auto log in feature
  Mail 197
auto repeat speed 26, 32
autodial option 178
autoexec.bat 88